Armour's Monthly Cook Book

Edited by Mary Jane McClure

Armour's Monthly Cook Book

· A Monthly Magazine
Of Household Interest ·

VOL. II NO. 12.
OCTOBER 1913.

Armour's Monthly CookBook

A Monthly Magazine Of Household Interest—.

A Magazine Devoted to the Interests of Women

VOL. II NO. 12

OCTOBER 1913.

CONTENTS

The Garden in October

October is a fine time to plant every kind of "bulb, root and tuber," also all deciduous plants and shrubs, except those with thin bark or thick, fleshy roots (e.g., birch magnolia).

Clean up and burn diseased plants, manure the garden, plow it and leave it all winter.

Burn asparagus tops and manure the bed. Also make new asparagus and rhubarb beds and plant sets of extra early pearl onions for use next March. Put some parsley plants in a box and place it in a light cellar or in a shed.

Put some frozen rhubarb roots in a barrel of earth in the cellar where they will produce "pie-plant," for winter use. Dig chickory for salad and store in sand in a dry cellar. Blanch endive by tying lightly at the tips.

Pull up cabbages, leaving roots on, and stand upside down on shelf in cellar. Pick cranberries this month. Then cover the bog with a foot of water to drown bugs and to protect from frost. Rake up the fallen leaves and use as a mulch for flowers and shrubs. Hardwood leaves like oak and chestnut contain more plant food than those from soft wooded trees.—*Garden and Farm Almanac. Doubleday, Page and Company.*

Every Morning

A Little Crystal of Thought for Every Day in the Week

SUNDAY.

Most of us could manage to be fairly happy if we really tried to make the best of things.

MONDAY.

Don't get depressed even if things do seem to be going wrong at the moment. Depression will make matters worse rather than better. If you do your duty faithfully, the sun is sure to shine again sometime.

TUESDAY.

Many people pride themselves on their plain speaking. An ability to put things pleasantly is really far more valuable. Even fault-finding can be pleasantly done.

WEDNESDAY.

It always seems to me that God is probably less anxious that we should fulfil our tasks in life than that we should do our best.

THURSDAY.

Of the people who complain most bitterly that they have "no chance" probably a very small proportion would do great things if great opportunities came. "No chance" is a very old excuse.

FRIDAY.

Don't give way to selfishness—that detestable vice that we all find it so difficult to forgive in others.

SATURDAY.

Even if you don't like your work, try to do it well. It may lead on to your true vocation.

For the Automobile Visitor

It is the frequent experience of the housewife living in the country or suburbs these days to receive unexpected visits from friends who are touring in automobiles, and she finds she must have something attractive, dainty and nourishing ready at a moment's notice to supplement the cup of tea or coffee so welcome after a hot, dusty trip. It is a wise plan to keep a variety of Summer Sausage on hand, as in a very few minutes delicious sandwiches may be prepared with this, these sandwiches having the charm of novelty. It is impossible to deal in a short article with the many varieties of Summer Sausage, but there are three or four which can be touched upon. To have a thorough understanding of their goodness one must not only read about them but taste them. They are the staple diet in many foreign countries and in the Armour brand the native flavoring has been done with remarkable faithfulness—so much so that large quantities are shipped from this country every week to the countries where they originated.

CERVELAT: This sausage is made of finest pork chopped fine, smoked and air dried. It is highly spiced. A very delicious way to serve this is to cut thin slices of white bread in rounds just the size of the sausage. Put the meat, cut very thin, between the slices of bread and toast for a minute with a very hot fire. This keeps the exposed sides absolutely dry and the sandwich can be eaten without a fork.

GERMAN SALAMI: This sausage will be much appreciated by people who like the smoky flavor of ham and bacon. In it the meat is chopped a little coarser than in the Cervelat, and the spicing is the same as that used in Germany. Serve cut very thin, with rye or bran bread.

LACKSCHINKEN: This is a very delicately flavored German titbit. It is made of boneless pork loins cured in mild sweet pickle before smoking. It makes delicious sandwiches with white or brown bread sliced thin and lightly buttered.

MORTADELLA, a favorite Italian sausage, is made from lean pork ham meat chopped very fine. The flavoring is delicious, the careful blending of spices giving a distinctly foreign touch.

In many restaurants throughout the country they serve, as in foreign countries, a slice or two of Summer Sausage as an appetizer before beginning the meal. This custom is rapidly spreading into the home, and Summer Sausage now has an established place in the daily bill of fare.

All true work is sacred; in all work, were it but true hand labour, there is something of divineness.—CARLYLE.

Editorial

In Germany the government maintains a system of education in what is called intensive farming. Through instructors who go about the country, the farmers are taught how to get a bigger yield from the same area of soil. The work of these wonderful teachers is supplemented by women domestic science teachers who in the same manner visit the homes in their districts and instruct the good *Haus Frau* on how to improve, economize, and systematize in kitchen and household work.

The manner in which these women instruct is, I am sure, of especial interest to the Cook Book readers, inasmuch as the method is in a way practically the same as what the Cook Book is doing. Where they teach by hand and mouth the Cook Book has taught through its exchange of ideas, contest stories, and recipe contests, the object being the same in both cases that of instruction, education and economy in the kitchen and saving of steps in the housework.

It is truly said of Germans that they are the most frugal and economical of all people. In the past the usual method has been to exert this frugality with what is already on hand in the larder left-overs, so to speak. One point of the modern instruction of these wandering domestic science teachers, as they go from home to home, is to show the economy of systematic buying of groceries, meats and vegetables. Where the practice in the past has been to buy a little, so there is not much expenditure of money, German housewives are now taught the economy of buying in bulk, because it is cheaper, and there is never any waste of food in a German home, no matter how much of it there may be on hand.

Neither is there any good reason why there should be any waste of food in an American home. Economy or frugality comes from knowing how, and not from any stingy purpose, as some ill-advised people think.

The methods of these teachers show that this wonderful nation is alive to the fact that the high cost of living is in our own waste and carelessness, that oftentimes we do not make the most of what we have or what we are given to do with.

Mary Jane McClure

The Subject of Desserts

Although a meal satisfies your hunger you should have dessert, because the educated palate craves that particular spice as a proper finish. Scientists tell us that a dinner digests better because of a tasty dessert, which, they say, gives the final stimulus necessary to dispose of the food previously received.

The simple desserts are the best desserts, and none is more pleasing to the eye and the palate or so easily made or so frequently served in an imperfect manner, than custards.

With a supply of good eggs in the pantry the housewife need never be at a loss for a tasty custard, and if she is wise enough to buy Armour's Fancy Selects when she orders eggs from her market man their goodness will be reflected in her desserts. Aside from their goodness their extra large size will always recommend their use to the wise housewife. They come packed in an extra large carton.

Custard Puddings

These being the more easily made may be considered first. They may either be steamed or baked but the mixture is the same in either case. Allow two eggs and a teaspoonful of sugar to each half pint of milk. Beat the eggs with sugar thoroughly, but do not froth them, as the custard must be as smooth and free from holes as possible. Add the milk slowly, also a few drops of flavoring essence — vanilla, almonds or lemon. Pour into a buttered mould (or into individual moulds), set in a pan of hot water and bake until firm. Chill thoroughly and turn out on serving dish. Serve with sugar and cream. A pleasing addition to the above is made by garnishing the sides of the mould with strips of Canton ginger before pouring in the custard.

Coffee Custard

Make an infusion of coffee by pouring half a pint of boiling milk on a heaping tablespoonful of powdered coffee. Put it aside to settle, and when cold strain off the milk and use with the eggs as in previous recipe.

Boiled Custard

This is also made from milk and eggs and is usually served instead of cream with stewed or preserved fruit. "Boiled" custard is rather a misnomer as on no account must the boiling point be reached in cooking, for if the custard bubbles it curdles. As soon as the custard begins to thicken the saucepan must be taken from the fire and the stirring continued for a second or two longer. If the cooking is done in a double boiler the risk of boiling is very much lessened.

Everyday Uses of Armour's Grape Juice

Give your family Armour's Grape Juice as an everyday beverage and their bodies will be kept healthy without drugs.

Instead of serving fruit in the morning serve a wineglassful of Armour's Grape Juice undiluted. If taken at the beginning of breakfast do not add ice. For children, water may be added if desired.

In moistening mincemeat use Armour's Grape Juice instead of jelly or wine. In making "Brown Betty" use Armour's Grape Juice instead of water and molasses and you will find it richer and more delicious.

In making sauce for all kinds of fruit puddings, use Armour's Grape Juice, hot or cold, thickened when necessary with a little cornstarch.

When making fruit salad to be served as a dessert, pour over the mixed fruits, immediately before serving, a cup of Armour's Grape Juice.

In serving grape fruit, after carefully removing the white pith, pour over each portion a wineglassful of Armour's Grape Juice.

Many people find it difficult to take raw eggs when recommended by their doctor. This difficulty is removed by breaking the egg into a glass of Armour's Grape Juice. The egg is swallowed easily and in addition to the nourishment obtained there is the tonic value of the rich fruit from which the grape juice is taken.

The Sweet Places

I want to go back to the sweet mysterious places,
The crook in the creek-bed nobody knew but me,
Where the roots in the bank thrust out strange knotty faces,
Scaring the squirrels who stole there timidly.

I want to lie under the corn and hear it rustle,
  Cool and green in a long, straight, soldierly row,
I am tired of white-faced women and men of iron.
  I want to go back where the country grasses grow.

To the well-remembered pasture's shadiest corner,
  Where under the trees the wild ferns wove their laces;
Hearing the whip-poor-will's voice in its strange, rich sadness —
  I want to go back to the old beloved places.

Unafraid

Sleep lifts the flower-soul with gentle hand,
  And breathes upon it till the petals close
  Softly and drowsily; and, faint, there grows
A melody from some far shining strand.
The waking vision's holden to, till, fanned
  By vagrant winds from distant ports, it blows
  The singing lips of dreams into the rose.
The white Night leans to kiss the nodding land.
Thus, in a kindred way, will Brother Death
At the appointed hour let fall his breath
Upon my soul, which such kind dreamlessness
Of pillowing, after Life's storm and stress.
I shall lie unafraid, my petals furled,
To bloom anew within some fairer world.
—EXCHANGE

To Bleach White Silk

When either white silk fabric or embroidery has become yellowed from careless washing, it may be bleached in the following manner:

Dissolve two ounces each of salt and oxalic acid in six quarts of cold water.

4

Soak the silk in this until the yellow tinge disappears. This will take about an hour in ordinary cases.

Rinse immediately in several clear waters.

VERIBEST CANNED MEATS—save work and worry

Informal Porch Suppers

If you are fortunate enough to possess a wide porch or a stretch of lawn do not forget your less fortunate friends, and give an occasional informal party there while the weather is still fine. Food always tastes so much better in the fresh air and when friends are present it makes the affair nothing more than a kind of glorified picnic. There are few more pleasant ways of entertaining than by giving a porch party. It is very little trouble to arrange an affair of this kind—less than the average picnic indeed—and grown people usually enjoy it more as it is much more comfortable to sit in a chair before a real table than to perch on a log or rock while eating. A porch party is an ideal way of entertaining for the woman who has to do her own work. Most of the dishes can be prepared the day before, making the serving easier.

If not convenient to have a large table a number of small card tables placed close together will answer the purpose. Charming table sets of white crepe paper can be bought for very little and save very materially in the doing up of the linen.

Prepare as much as possible early in the day. If you have sandwiches wrap them in a damp napkin; if cold drinks are wanted have them well chilled, your glasses and straws handy, have your silver and china ready at hand so that when your guests arrive you may devote your time and attention to them. The following menus are not hard to prepare and the dishes will be found most palatable and suited to every purse: Veribest Canned Meats, the standby of the housewife who combines economy of time with excellence of quality, are used in many of them. There is a wide range of these meats delicious and many ways of using them. Every pantry should have at least one shelf devoted to them so that the housewife need never be at a loss for the basis of a good meal.

FRUIT COCKTAIL

HAM MOUSSÉ, POTATO CHIPS

or

CREAMED CHICKEN, served in roll,

or

TONGUE TOAST, CREAM SAUCE

or

CHICKEN IN ASPIC IN INDIVIDUAL MOULDS

POTATOES AU GRATIN

TOMATO WAFFLES

SALAD ROLLS

CHILLED CUCUMBERS

MARSHMALLOW PUDDING

or

FIG CUSTARD

COFFEE FRAPPÉ ICED COCOA

GRAPE JUICE.

Ham Moussé

One tablespoonful granulated gelatine, one half cup hot water, one can Veribest Deviled Ham, teaspoonful mustard (mixed), one half cup rich cream.

Dissolve the gelatine in the hot water, and add to the ham; season with the mustard, add the cream beaten stiff and pour into a mould which has been previously wet with cold water. Chill. Turn out to serve and garnish with parsley.

Creamed Chicken

Make a plain white sauce of one tablespoonful butter, one tablespoonful flour and one cup of milk with seasoning of salt and pepper. When this is ready add the contents of a can of Veribest Boned Chicken, gently pulling apart the flakes of meat with a fork. When thoroughly heated serve in a roll which has been hollowed out for the purpose, with a garnish of cooked asparagus stalks.

Tongue Toast

Remove the contents of a can of Veribest Lunch Tongue and cut in dice. Add a little cream and the beaten yolk of one egg. Simmer for a few minutes and serve on squares of toast.

Potatoes au Gratin

Dice enough cold boiled potatoes to measure one pint. Put one tablespoonful of butter and the same amount of flour in a saucepan with a little salt and pepper. Cook till well mixed, then add one cupful of milk and stir until smooth and thick. Add the potatoes and simmer five minutes, then pour into a buttered, shallow baking dish. Mix one scant cupful of fine, dry bread crumbs with one tablespoonful of melted butter, spread over the potatoes and place in a hot oven until the crumbs are a golden brown, then serve hot.

Marshmallow Pudding

Make a plain lemon jelly, adding a little sherry wine if desired. Put a layer of sliced marshmallows in the bottom of the mold, and when the jelly has begun to set spread a little of it over them. Continue with jelly and marshmallows till the mold is full, then put away to harden. Serve with whipped cream.

A Dainty Dessert

Lemon and grape juice frappé is another cool dessert that is also light. To make it, boil a pint of water with two cupfuls of granulated sugar for ten minutes and cool it. Then add a little cinnamon and half a cupful of lemon juice, and lastly a quart of Armour's grape juice. Freeze and serve in cups, with a little of the grape juice.

Shelving Responsibility

"I'll ask my husband."

"I don't think my husband would allow me to do that."

"I'm sure Jack would say 'No.'"

Do you know the wife who, whenever she does not want to do anything, always places the responsibility on her husband's shoulders?

She knows quite well that she can do almost anything she likes with her husband, and that there are really precious few things that he *would* say "No" to her doing, but she finds that to say her husband would never allow her to do this, or that, is a very easy way of saying "No" to people without offending them.

But it's not quite fair on the husband really, because, after a time, people begin to think that he really must be rather a bear to be so strict with his wife.

And he gets disliked, very often, accordingly.

If you don't want to do a thing, *say* so; don't make your husband the scapegoat.

Of course the wife who does this kind of thing never dreams that people will blame her husband: it's just a convenient fiction to her.

But people are apt to think less of her husband because of it.

So you'll be wise to find some other excuse when excuses are necessary.—*Exchange.*

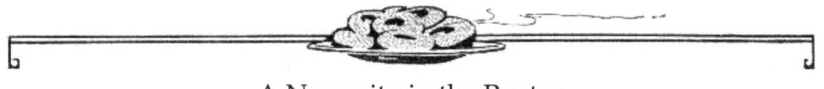

A Necessity in the Pantry

"How can you get along without a ham in the house?" asked one housewife of another; "to me it is as necessary as anything we ever have in our pantry."

This housewife, in saying the above, echoed the sentiments of many others. There is no meat more "necessary" in the house than good ham. Not only is the meat there in all its nutriment but it is preserved—that is, cured and smoked—in such a way that there is given to it a piquancy which whets the appetite and gives a stimulus to the gastric juices, thus aiding—so the doctors tell us—the process of digestion.

In so many cases of convalescence where the appetite is flagging and the digestion weak, ham and bacon are prescribed, both for their tonic and nutritive value.

On the crisp snappy mornings of autumn when a hearty breakfast is necessary and the appetite has not yet recovered from the jading effects of the hot weather what could be more tempting and more nourishing than a slice of broiled ham—broiled just enough to be thoroughly cooked and yet not enough to discolor the delicious appetising pink color of the meat. Even the aroma thrown out in the process of cooking sends a tempting appeal to the stomach that is impossible to resist.

Buying a whole ham at a time is the best and most economical way of buying ham, as experience will prove. It can be boiled or baked whole and sliced for whatever purpose intended. When baked ham is broiled for breakfast it requires to be cooked just long enough to get hot all the way through.

It is many years since the curing of ham was first tried and in those years much has been accomplished. Today Armour's Star Hams represent perfection in cured ham. In them the highest quality is allied to skillful curing and careful smoking.

From many thousand hams those intended for the Star brand are chosen; the process of curing is a specialty of Armour and Company, and careful smoking over green hickory logs gives the final necessary touch.

They say "the proof of the pudding is the tasting of it" and this applies to Armour's Star Hams as well.

[Many ways of using this, to most people, necessary meat, will be found on page 34.]

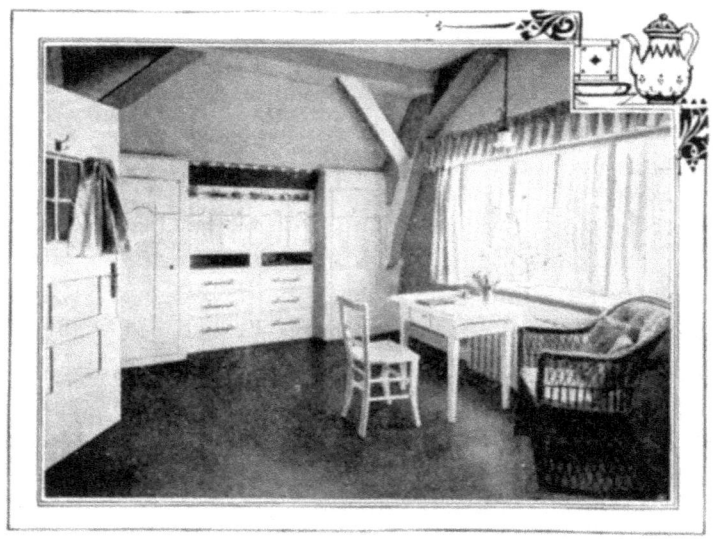

Built in Cupboards and Shelves Economize on Space and are
Especially Nice for Linens

Halloween Hints

Witch Apples

Bake large apples from which the core has been removed until soft, but not long enough to burst the skin. When cooked, insert a marshmallow into the core space, put a teaspoonful of sugar on top and a few maraschino cherries. When ready to serve turn over each a scant teaspoonful of brandy and light just as the table is reached. The brandy will burn with a ghastly flame and melt the sugar and marshmallows. Whipped cream served in a bowl is a delicious addition.

Witch Cake

Cream one half cupful of butter with one and one half cupfuls of sugar; add three eggs and beat five minutes; add one cupful of milk. Sift together one third cupful of cornstarch, and two cupfuls of flour, one and one half teaspoonfuls of ground mixed spices, and three teaspoonfuls of baking powder; then add to the mixture. Now add one cupful of seeded floured raisins, also one cupful of chopped nuts. Turn into a well greased loaf cake pan and bake in a moderate oven about forty-five minutes. Frost with a white boiled icing. Melt sweet chocolate to equal one third cupful, flavor with a teaspoonful of lemon juice, add one cupful of boiled chestnuts which have been run through the meat grinder, and enough confectionery sugar to make a paste easily handled. Roll and cut (by pasteboard pattern) black cats or any other Halloween figure, press them into the icing on the sides of the cake.

Sautéing and Frying

"What is the difference between sautéing potatoes and frying them?" asks a young housekeeper from South Dakota in the Day's Work, and as the subject is of much importance and deserving of more space than may be given to it in the correspondence columns it is answered here.

In a word, to sauté—pronounced sotay—anything, is to cook it in a shallow frying pan with a little fat, turning as one side is browned to let the other color. Cooked potatoes are often warmed over this way. To "fry" potatoes, croquettes, etc., is to cook them in deep boiling fat, immersing the object to be fried while the fat is boiling hot.

That is the difference between sautéing and frying but there are one or two points about frying—this much abused way of cooking—that must be borne in mind if one would have the best results. In frying, a deep kettle must be used and it is wise to keep one for this purpose only. The one called a Scotch bowl is especially made for this purpose and is most satisfactory.

Use only the best fat for frying—an absolutely pure leaf lard which contains neither water nor salt and have your kettle two thirds full, that is, deep enough to quite cover the article to be fried. Once started, this quantity must be kept up, as it reduces slightly with each frying, but the same fat may be used again and again if care be taken to keep it clean and of a good color. After each frying let the fat cool a little and strain to remove crumbs, etc., which would otherwise burn and spoil the fat. If strained when very hot it is apt to unsolder the strainer. Wipe the kettle clean, return the strained lard and set aside until wanted again.

French Fried Potatoes are sliced thin or cut lengthwise in strips laid in ice water for half an hour; then dried thoroughly between two towels and plunged into boiling deep fat. As soon as they are delicately browned they are fished out with a split spoon and laid in a hot colander to drain off every drop of fat. Serve at once.

German Fried Potatoes are as a rule cooked and cold before they are sautéed. Some prefer them to the French. To many minds they never get quite rid of the stale taste that clings to the cold potato. The same may be said of stewed cold, cooked potatoes. The least objectionable way of serving them as left-overs is to sauté them.

Simple Furniture of Quaint Shape and Design

"To have bread excite thankfulness, and a drink of water send the heart to God, is better than sighs for the unattainable. To plough a straight furrow on Monday, or dust a room well on Tuesday, or kiss a bumped forehead on Wednesday, is worth more than the most ecstatic thrill under Sunday eloquence. Spirituality is seeing God in common things and showing God in common tasks." —MALTBIE D. BACOCK.

The School Child's Sleep

The mother who has a child at school may not be able to help him with his lessons, but there is one thing she can do for him which will benefit him even more, and that is to see that he gets enough sleep.

Insufficient sleep affects the nerves, the temper, the digestion, the mental quickness, and even the morals of children. The child who gets enough sleep is the one who is bright and quick mentally, who grows normally and well, who eats properly and who is not peevish and irritable.

An early supper and an early bedtime are the things for the school child. Then put him in a well-ventilated bedroom and let him have ten or eleven full hours of slumber and he'll wake up bright and healthy and good, too.

Many of the little whining nervous children we see are simply suffering from lack of sleep. Many small naughtinesses simply come from tired nerves and weariness of mind and body. So many mothers notice such a difference in the behavior of children once they have started to school and are at a loss to understand the reason. It is because the daily nap which the child took before he went to school has been given up, but the bedtime hour has not been changed. Consequently the nerves of the child suffer.

Try giving the school child supper at half past five, a nourishing and easily digested supper, too. Then at eight, promptly pack him off to bed. If he doesn't sleep let him sip a cup of hot milk, and sit beside him until he drowses off. Sleep is largely a habit and will be easily acquired in a few evenings. And oh, the difference it will make to the child in every way.—*Exchange.*

Hints on Picture Hanging

Hang the pictures from the ceiling or picture rail by means of a thin cord as nearly as possible the color of the walls. When this is done you may, if you like, fill up the spaces left above the smaller pictures by placing therein a miniature, or an old blue plate, or a little plaster relief. This arrangement gives all the space, above or below, upon which to rest your eyes, and is infinitely preferable to the usual way of hanging pictures one over the other or all up and down the walls. Fishing line makes an excellent substitute for picture wire and is much less conspicuous.

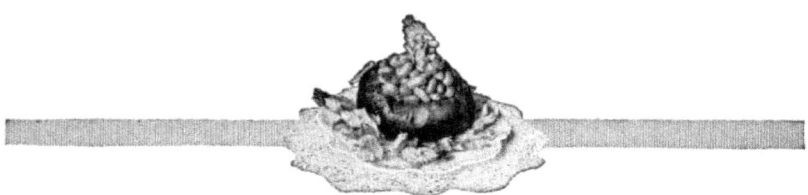

From the Pantry Shelf

Keeping the pantry shelf supplied with foods that are easily prepared and served is one of the things which mark the careful housewife. The Veribest list of prepared foods embraces soups, meats, baked beans and many varieties of potted ham, veal, chicken, etc., all of which are perfect. Their use means a saving of time, fuel and energy—with satisfaction for the whole family.

CHICKEN MOUSSÉ

One cup of chicken stock (made from Armour's Chicken Bouillon Cubes), one half teaspoon of salt, a pinch of celery salt, one cup of Armour's Veribest Boned Chicken, two teaspoons of granulated gelatine, two tablespoons of cold water, one cup of beaten cream, one tablespoon of chopped olives, and whites of two eggs. Heat the stock, seasoning and gelatine which has been soaked in cold water. When dissolved, add the chicken finely minced with fork, and the cream. Beat well and fold in the well-beaten whites of eggs. Pour into buttered molds and chill for two or three hours. Serve as salad with mayonnaise.—MRS. A. E. RICHESON, 830 CANAL ST., MT. VERNON, IND.

CHICKEN AND MACARONI

Put one half package of macaroni in boiling salted water and boil until tender. Drain off all but a very little water and add grated cheese. Stir well, cover and keep hot until the cheese is melted. Have ready a cream sauce made from milk, flour and butter, and when hot add one can of Armour's Veribest Boned Chicken. Mix the macaroni and creamed chicken lightly, and serve on buttered hot toast.—MRS. H. B. HILL, SARVER, PA.

CASSEROLE OF RICE AND BEEF

One can of Armour's Veribest Roast Beef, one half teaspoon of salt, one fourth teaspoon of pepper, one egg, one tablespoon of chopped parsley, one fourth cup of fine bread crumbs and three cups of cooked rice. Season the meat and mix with crumbs and egg. Add just enough stock to bind. Make stock of one fourth teaspoon of Armour's Extract of Beef and one half cup of hot water. Line a mold with half the rice. Fill with the seasoned meat and cover with the remainder of the rice. Cover tightly and steam thirty minutes. Serve with tomato sauce. — MRS. FRANK GROUNDWATER, ELMA, WASH.

JELLIED VEAL

Make a rich gravy by browning one tablespoon of flour in one tablespoon of Armour's Simon Pure Leaf Lard, and add one large onion cut fine, one fresh tomato or tomato pulp, and one teaspoon of Armour's Extract of Beef. Season with salt and pepper and let the gravy simmer until it thickens, then add one can of Veribest Veal Loaf, and mix it thoroughly in the gravy. Dissolve a package of gelatine in boiling water and mix it thoroughly with the veal and gravy. Put aside to cool and then set it in refrigerator for a few hours. Slice and garnish with parsley and a few slices of lemon. — MRS. VIOLA MICHEL BODE, 2865 FORTIN STREET, NEW ORLEANS, LA.

MACARONI MILANAISE

Cook one half package of macaroni in three quarts of salted water (boiling) until tender. Drain well and cover with cold water for ten minutes or more. Cook one can of tomatoes for fifteen minutes with a bay leaf, a bit of mace, onion, cloves, parsley, salt and pepper. Strain and thicken with one fourth cup each of butter and flour blended together. Drain macaroni again and mix with the sauce. Add one cup of chopped green peppers parboiled, and one can of Veribest Tongue chopped, and put in baking dish. Sprinkle top with grated cheese or buttered cracker crumbs and bake one half hour. — MRS. C. F. FRANKLIN, 214 NORTH UNION AVENUE, SHAWNEE, OKLA.

CREAMED CHIPPED BEEF ON TOAST

One half can of Armour's Veribest Chipped Beef, two tablespoons of cornstarch, a little paprika, one and one half cups of milk, and three fourths cup of tomato catsup. Heat the milk and add the cornstarch which has previously been moistened with cold water, add the paprika, and stir until thickened. Then add catsup, stir in the beef and let it become thoroughly heated. Serve on hot buttered toast. — EDITH EVELYN RUNGE, 15TH AVE. AND RAY ST., SPOKANE, WASH.

ITALIAN TONGUE

Slice one Veribest Canned Tongue and pour over it the following sauce: Put one half cup of olive oil in a sauce pan and when hot add one pint of tomatoes, a teaspoon of salt, twelve olives pitted and cut in two, one bayleaf, two cloves, one fourth cup of chopped raisins. Let boil, then simmer forty-five minutes. Pour over the tongue and serve. — MRS. L. R. FINK, NEW ULM, TEXAS.

SCALLOPED TONGUE

One cup of brown sauce, made with Armour's Extract of Beef, one can of Veribest Ox Tongue, split, one half cup of buttered crumbs, one tablespoon of catsup, one teaspoon of Worcestershire Sauce. Sprinkle baking dish with crumbs, and arrange the split tongues in dish. Pour over them the sauce to which catsup and Worcestershire Sauce have been added. Cover with the remainder of the crumbs and bake in hot oven until the crumbs are brown. — MRS. C. B. COLPITTS, KANSAS CITY, MO.

LUNCHEON DISH

Split and broil Veribest Vienna Style Sausage and place between hot buttered toast. Add a crisp, dry lettuce leaf and a thin spread of mayonnaise. Serve in folded napkin with olives and sweet pickles. — MRS. R. F. THURSTON, 2717 26TH AVENUE, FRUITVALE, CAL.

BEEF BALLS

Two cans of Armour's Veribest Potted Meat, one onion minced very fine, three cups of mashed potato, salt and pepper to season, and one egg. Beat well and form into balls. Roll them in flour and fry in deep hot Simon Pure Leaf Lard. Garnish with parsley or lettuce leaves and serve hot.—MRS. M. E. BESSEY, 133 MAIN ST., BILOXI, MISS.

HASH WITH SPANISH SAUCE

With one can of Armour's Veribest Corn Beef Hash mix one cup of boiled potatoes chopped fine. Season to taste and sauté in hot Simon Pure Lard until brown, and pour over the following sauce: Boil together for ten minutes one can of Armour's Veribest Tomato Soup, one half can of shredded pimentoes, one half can of button mushrooms; season with salt, paprika, butter and a small amount of onion juice.—MRS. J. M. AINGELL, 2704 NUECES, AUSTIN, TEXAS.

CALGARIAN SALAD

Chop one tin of Armour's Veribest Boned Chicken. To this add one cucumber pared and cubed, one cup of chopped walnuts, one half cup of French peas, one cup of celery washed, scraped and cut into small pieces. Moisten with mayonnaise, mold in bowl, mask with dressing. Garnish with strips of canned red peppers and celery tips.—MRS. G. B. CONTTS, CALGARY, ALBERTA, CANADA.

"Kissing don't last; Cookery do."—GEORGE MEREDITH.

Saving Steps in the Kitchen

The kitchen should be characterized by cleanliness, system and order. Two maxims that will help save steps are: "A place for everything, and everything in its place;" and "Plan your work, then work your plan."

1. Arrange kitchen as conveniently and systematically as possible. Walls and floors should be easily cleaned. No superfluous furnishings or worn-out utensils should be tolerated. Arrange stove, sink, shelves, table or kitchen cabinet near together and in logical order, so that in preparing a dish one can move from raw material at table or cabinet around to the washed dish at sink. Have shelves and hooks within easy reach. Have drain-board and shelves for dishes convenient to sink. Keep stove lifters and cloths for managing hot dishes upon hooks near stove. Arrange those utensils and raw materials in constant use close at hand, placing utensils used in same kind of work together. In storeroom and pantry arrange shelves in certain order, with things seldom used on highest shelves and those used oftener on lower shelves. Place together ingredients used for salad-making, as vinegar, mustard, etc.; things used in laundry together, etc. Other groups will suggest themselves. Keep all groceries possible in air-tight labelled cans or glass jars.

2. Stock your kitchen with as many labor-saving devices as you can afford, making sure they are suited to your needs. Keep all utensils and tools in good repair. Glass oven-doors, small tables upon rollers which can be wheeled into dining room, indexed cook books and clipping-files are step-savers.

3. Plan each day's work ahead and have materials and utensils for that day's work handy.

4. Do all kitchen work in a certain order, using that routine which experience has proved best.

5. Think before you step. When in storeroom or pantry bring as many needed articles as possible at one time. Baskets and waiters are great helps here. In preparing a certain dish first gather together all necessary ingredients and utensils. Do not begin work until everything is ready. When possible prepare several things for the stove at once.

6. Clean and straighten as you go, replacing disarranged utensils, etc. Have plenty of hot water handy, placing in soak those articles which cannot be washed immediately. While preparing one meal do as much as possible toward getting the next ready. If meals are planned ahead, many things for supper can be cooked with the noon-day meal, also the breakfast cereal. After each meal leave everything ship-shape for the next.

Mrs. L. H. McRaven, Meridian, Miss.

> *"Nobody knows the work it takes*
> *To keep the home together;*
> *Nobody knows the steps it takes,*
> *Nobody knows but Mother."*

Keep a small market basket handy. In it place the things to be taken upstairs when you are going up and when you are making the beds and dusting, the things which are to be brought down.

"Make your head save your heels." Think, in making trips to pantry, cellar or icebox if you cannot both take things and bring others on the same trip.

Keep a chair or revolving stool in the kitchen and whenever possible sit down to work. Vegetable paring, cake beating and even washing and ironing may be done sitting.

Have a method in your work. Occasionally take time to sit down and think over the day's work, and remember how many unnecessary steps you took yesterday.

Have your kitchen shelves arranged to suit your own height, so that there is no unnecessary straining to reach up or bending over to reach one set too low.

Supplying the Meat Flavor

There are many meat dishes very nourishing and wholesome which are total failures because of their lack of flavor. This lack of flavor seriously impairs their value in nutriment. A little Armour's Extract of Beef will in every case provide that touch of flavor which appeals to the palate and finds ready response from the digestive juices of the stomach. This extract is very highly concentrated, so that only a little is required.

RICE SOUP

Dissolve one teaspoon of Armour's Extract of Beef in one quart of water, add one half cup of cooked rice, and a tablespoon of onion juice. Add one teaspoon of celery seed and cover closely. Simmer ten minutes and just before serving add one fourth cup of sweet cream or a tablespoon of butter. If too thick, add a little boiling water or milk.—-MRS. W. V. COPELAND, 227 N. LAKE STREET, TOPEKA, KANS.

SPINACH AND SAUCE

After spinach has boiled for twenty minutes in salt water, drain it and serve with this sauce: Dissolve one half teaspoon of Armour's Extract of Beef in a cup of hot water, add two tablespoons of butter, break in two eggs and use half teaspoon of lemon juice. Stir constantly and cook for a few minutes.—MRS. W. I. COLE, PUNTA GORDA, FLA.

TOMATO ASPIC JELLY

One fourth teaspoon of Armour's Extract of Beef, one can of Veribest Tomato Soup, one half package of gelatine, three hard-boiled eggs, and chopped olives. Heat the soup with an equal amount of water. Soak the gelatine in half cup of cold water and dissolve in the soup.

Add Extract of Beef dissolved in a little water. Let cool. Add chopped hard boiled eggs and olives. If there is cold chicken at hand, a half cup of chicken chopped will improve the jelly. Pour into mold and put on ice. Serve with mayonnaise on lettuce leaves.—MRS. R. M. BRUMBY, ANONA, FLA.

STUFFED TOMATOES

Remove seeds and centers from six tomatoes. Chop three green peppers and one onion and fry in butter until the onions begin to brown. Add a small lump of butter, some chopped nuts and dried bread crumbs, salt and pepper to season, and one third cup of hot water in which one half teaspoon of Armour's Extract of Beef has been dissolved. Put the tomatoes in baking pan and fill with this mixture. Sprinkle crumbs over tops and bake fifteen minutes.—MRS. L. C. STUMP, 444 N. DENVER AVE., KANSAS CITY, MO.

BREAD OMELET

Cut one cup of stale bread into tiny bits, beat the yolks of two eggs, add a pint of milk and the crumbs. Season with a pinch of salt and pepper and one half teaspoon of Armour's Extract of Beef. Let stand ten minutes, and then sauté in Armour's Simon Pure Leaf Lard until a nice brown. Add the whites whipped just a moment before taking from the fire.—ELLA R. STAHL, ROUNDUP, MONT.

FRIED ONIONS

Into a small amount of hot butter slice six good-sized green onions, tops and all. Cook until wilted, add a little water and boil until it has evaporated. Scramble in a spoonful of Armour's Beef Extract, three eggs, pepper and salt to taste. Cook until creamy and serve hot.— MRS. OLLIE H. THOMAS, MANSFIELD, ARK.

MUSHROOM SAUCE

Use the liquor from one can of mushrooms and enough water to make one cupful. Chop the mushrooms, add one teaspoon of Armour's Extract of Beef, and slightly thicken with flour blended with water. Cook six minutes and serve with broiled steak.—GRACE M. SEARS.

PEA SOUP

One can of peas, one half teaspoon of Armour's Extract of Beef, two tablespoons of butter, one tablespoon of flour, one teaspoon of salt and a dash of pepper, one half teaspoon of sugar, one quart of milk or half milk and half cream. Rinse the peas, add some water and boil until soft, then rub through a colander. Add Armour's Extract of Beef to hot water and peas, making one quart in all. Melt the butter and add the flour, then gradually the hot soup. Cook until smooth, add the seasoning, and the milk and cream last.—KATHERINE SORLIE, Buxton, N. Dak.

CORN SOUP

Cook in two tablespoons of butter one onion and one sprig of parsley (cut fine) for five minutes. Add one cup of chopped corn and a cup of hot water in which has been dissolved one half teaspoon of Armour's Extract of Beef. Cook fifteen minutes. Add salt, pepper, one cup of milk, and bind with two tablespoons of flour and butter blended. Serve with toasted croutons.—MISS AMANDA STEVENS, South Lee, N. H.

JELLIED BOUILLON SALAD

Make a clear bouillon, using one teaspoon of Armour's Extract of Beef to one pint of hot water. Dissolve one spoon of powdered gelatine and stir into the hot liquid. Stir in a few button mushrooms sliced, or some cold veal. Add the pulp of one orange, having it peeled, sliced and torn in sections. When cool turn into cups or molds moistened with cold water. Stir and divide the material about equal in each cup. Set on ice to harden. Slice firm tomatoes and lay one each on lettuce leaf. Turn the bouillon molds onto these and place a large spoon of dressing over each.—MRS. SADETTE HARRINGTON, Elkhorn, Wis.

EGG SANDWICHES

Mash six hard-boiled eggs very fine, adding pepper, salt and a small lump of butter. Mix with one half teaspoon of Armour's Extract of Beef dissolved in a tablespoon of hot water, and one third cup of mayonnaise dressing. Add one cup of finely chopped pecans or peanuts. Mix well and serve between fresh crackers and thin slices of bread.—NELLIE TONEY, 215 WEST CHURCH ST., GREENWOOD, MISS.

POTATO PUFFS

Bake four large potatoes and put them through potato ricer. Season with butter, salt and white pepper and add one half teaspoon of Armour's Extract of Beef. Beat into this the stiffly beaten white of one egg. Mold this well and roll out on molding board. Cut into cakes and place on buttered sheet. Bake in hot oven until a golden brown. Serve on platter with meat, garnished with cress or parsley. MISS S. MAY KIMBALL, 7 TAHANTO ST., CONCORD, N. H.

WILTED LETTUCE SALAD

Wash two heads of lettuce and lay them on ice until wanted, then cut in small bits and lay in salad dish, adding salt. Heat two tablespoons of olive oil and pour over the lettuce. To one half cup of white wine vinegar add one teaspoon of sugar, one half teaspoon of Armour's Extract of Beef, one tablespoon of mayonnaise dressing. Pour over the lettuce and garnish with slices of hard-boiled eggs.—LOUISE MALLOY, 464 BAYOU ST., BATESVILLE, ARK.

Armour's Star Ham—for half a century the best

Home Dressmaking

This is an age of good ready made clothes and it is also an age of clever amateur dressmaking. With excellent patterns which may be easily handled there is no reason why the woman who can sew should not make her own clothes, and have smart clothes at a reasonable price—that is, provided she has the time to give to sewing.

Before starting a dress—even before buying—make a tour of the shops and see for yourself what is being worn with a keen eye for the little details which lift a gown from the home made to the professional class. If you live far from town and can not go to the shops look through the magazines which make a feature of dress and study what is best suited to your particular style and requirements. Study materials and buy economically, which means paying a little more if necessary rather than have shoddy goods.

Good patterns are essential and these usually have full directions as to the manner of using. It is a very good plan to have a pattern drafted to your own measure but if you have not this take some finished garment which is satisfactory (unless there is someone at hand to take the measures that a person cannot very well take for herself) and measure the lengths in different places such as front, back and under lengths on a blouse and the width across both back and front where it is broadest. Write these down and proceed to take the same measures on the pattern to be used. In taking measures be sure to take a correct position or it will be impossible to get correct measures and you cannot hope for success if this—the initial step—is taken wrongly. For instance, stand erect with the chest raised and the abdomen held in and you will find in taking the width measures across to where the arms and body join the armhole will be straight and even looking instead of pointing in and out in places.

Make sure of your measures before starting to apply your pattern to the cloth. A careful study of this will save many irreparable mistakes later.

Halloween

The date of this oldtime celebration is always October 31st, the crucial moment 12 o'clock. To be sure, the original observance of All Hallows Eve has been considerably distorted during the course of years but the fun it affords the young folks in its present manner of keeping cannot be gainsaid and needs no changing. Halloween is the night when a magic spell enthrals the earth. Witches, bogies, brownies and elves are all abroad to use their power. Superstition proves true, witchery is recognized and the future may be read in a hundred and one ways.

No occasion gives more opportunity of enjoyment and no party is gayer than a Halloween party.

It is not necessary to spend a great deal of money in giving a Halloween party. With a little time, some suitable paper and a pair of sharp scissors the witches, pumpkin faces, cats and bats, which are the distinctive features of this decoration, may be easily made at home. Yellow, red and black are the colors and the most fascinating crepe paper can be had for a few cents. This is the best material to use, as it lends itself so well to all sorts of schemes.

Not only is it made in plain colors which may be decorated at will but for every festival and occasion there are special designs which make the work of decoration very easy indeed.

For Halloween there is a design of witches with brooms, or cats and bats in black on a yellow ground. This is ready to be laid on the table as a cover or around the room in the effect of a frieze. There are napkins to match and a crepe paper rope to finish the edge.

A weird effect of lighting is obtained by making lantern boxes from any discarded boxes which may be in the house. Cover them with crepe paper, cut eyes, nose, ears and mouth, paste colored tissue paper behind the features and set a lighted candle inside.

The wise owl must not be forgotten in the Halloween decorations. Grey paper is best for him. Paste the edges of a square piece of grey crepe paper together lengthwise of the grain and gather in at the bottom. Stuff this bag with soft paper or cotton and gather again some distance from the top. Shape the top into ears and make two rosettes with black centers for eyes. A beak of black stiff paper protrudes between the eyes. Mount the owl on a branch by sewing with heavy black thread in a way to resemble claws.

Make witches' brooms by tying slashed paper tied on any old sticks or brooms to give the effect.

How to Clean It

Brass Ornaments

Any brass which is exposed to the air is likely to tarnish very quickly. To obviate this, after I have cleaned and polished my brass vases etc., in the usual way I take a rag, and with this smear just a tiny scrap of vaseline over the brass. This keeps it bright and prevents it from tarnishing.

Wicker Tables or Chairs

To take stains out of white wicker-work, I get some oxalic acid, and with an old toothbrush dipped in this I brush the stained parts well. Then I rinse the article thoroughly, first in clear, warm water, and then in cold. The brush should be destroyed after use, as oxalic acid is poisonous.

To Wash Chiffon

To wash chiffon, wind the material round a bottle. Make a good lather of soap and water. Immerse the bottle, and move backwards and forwards in the lather for about five minutes. Rinse in clear, lukewarm water in which has been dissolved a small piece of gum arabic. Then unwind the chiffon, spread on the ironing board, lay a clean, thin cloth over it, and iron with a very hot iron.

A Black Hat

The very best way to clean a black hat, whether it be chip, mohair, or tagel, real or imitation, is to make some rather strong tea, and, after brushing all dust from the hat, apply this with a small brush. Saturate the hat thoroughly, and when dry it will be as perfect in colour and appearance as when first bought.

If you want the hat to be stiff, add half a teaspoonful of liquid gum to the tea, and mix well before applying. The hat will then keep its stiffness, but will not have a glossy appearance.

Real Lace

Real lace should never be washed, but can be cleaned in the following way. Put it between layers of tissue paper well sprinkled with calcined magnesia, place between the leaves of a book, and under a heavy weight for three days. Then shake the powder out and the lace will be perfectly clean.

Small Pieces from the Whole Ham

The economy of buying a whole ham at once instead of a pound or a slice is apparent to every housewife who studies her weekly bills. The initial cost is less—many trips to the store are saved and the housewife has the chance of using all of the ham—trimmings, skin, bone, etc., etc.

HAM TOAST

Grind or chop enough Armour's Star Ham to make a cupful, using a little of the fat. Melt one tablespoon of butter in a sauce pan and add one tablespoon of flour. As soon as blended add one and one third cups of milk. When slightly thickened add the ham and the whites of two hard-boiled eggs which have been mashed with fork. Season with salt, pepper, and pour over round slices of toast which have been placed on hot platter. Grate the yolks of eggs and sprinkle over the top. Garnish with parsley.—MRS. G. F. JONES, 79 WASHINGTON ST., PORTLAND, MAINE.

HAM DUMPLINGS

Cut from a boiled Star Ham fat and lean in equal proportions and chop fine. Season with pepper and minced sage. Make a crust of one half pound of Armour's Butterine and one pound of flour. Roll it out thick and divide it into equal portions. Put some ham into each and close up the crust. Have ready a pot of boiling water and put in the dumplings. Boil about forty-five minutes.—MISS M. C. GREEN, 319 LOCUST ST., HUNTSVILLE, ALA.

HAM RELISH

One cup of Armour's Star Ham boiled and chopped fine, one half cup of cream, three hard-boiled eggs, salt and pepper to taste. Scald the cream. Rub the yolks smooth with a little of the cream and add to the cream in the farina boiler with the ham. Press the whites of the two eggs through a sieve, add to the mixture and when thoroughly heated put on a hot dish. Slice the remaining eggs over the ham and serve.—MRS. R. SCHROEDER, 1923 AVENUE D, BIRMINGHAM, ALA.

ESCALLOPED HAM

Boil six eggs ten minutes. Make a thickening of two tablespoons of flour cooked in two tablespoons of melted butter, and boil it in a pint of milk until thick. Season with salt and pepper. Cut a cup of Armour's Star Ham (cold boiled) into dice and moisten half a cup of cracker crumbs in melted butter. Chop the whites of the eggs fine, sprinkle some crumbs in a buttered dish, then some of the ham, the chopped whites, thickened milk and sifted yolks. Then add the remainder of the ham, whites of eggs and milk, cover with buttered crumbs and bake until brown.—-ALMA E. EDDY, COLLEGE CITY, CAL.

BAKED LEFT-OVERS

One cup of Armour's Star Ham chopped fine, one half cup of bread crumbs and one half cup of chopped hard-boiled eggs. Season and stir into a thick gravy flavored with Armour's Extract of Beef. Bake and serve hot in pepper shells.—MRS. R. P. GARIG, PORT ARTHUR, TEXAS.

HAM MOLD

Three pounds of Armour's Star Ham, one cup of sweet milk, fifteen drops of lemon, salt and pepper to taste. Cut the meat in small pieces, cover the mold with a layer of slices of hard-boiled egg, then a layer of meat. Repeat until the mold is filled, then add cup of milk, one teaspoon of Armour's Extract of Beef, lemon, salt and pepper. Stir well and pour over the top. Bake a nice brown.—MRS. P. W. PINNELL, 131 WINDER STREET, HENDERSON, N. C.

HAM SOUFFLÉ

Beat three eggs until very light, add one cup of Armour's Star Ham (cooked and chopped), one half cup of bread crumbs, one pint of milk, pepper and salt. Mix thoroughly and bake thirty minutes.—MRS. LOUISE McCONNELL, 1115 CARLOS AVE., WICHITA, KANS.

HAM LOAF

Two cups of ground boiled Star Ham, one teaspoon of Armour's Extract of Beef, half a package of gelatine, one pint of water, salt and pepper to taste. Dissolve Beef Extract in one half pint of boiling water, season. Dissolve the gelatine in one half pint of cold water. Stand the vessel in hot water to dissolve it. Mix together with beef extract, set aside to cool. When this begins to harden, beat in the ground boiled ham, set mold in refrigerator. Serve in slices with bread and butter, sweet pickle or lettuce salad.—MRS. R. H. WEST, ALAMOGORDO, N. MEX.

HAM POTPIE

Take the bone of an Armour's Star Ham after the meat is partly used, and boil slowly until meat is tender. Slice three potatoes, take out the bone and put in potatoes while cooking. Make dumplings of three pints of flour, a pinch of salt and a big tablespoon of Armour's Simon Pure Leaf Lard. Mix with water, roll thin as pie crust and drop into broth.—MRS. NETTIE GARGAN, 715 SHERMAN ST., DENVER, COLO.

HASH WITH EGGS

One cup of Armour's Star Ham boiled and chopped fine, one cup of potato mashed, one cup of cracker or bread crumbs. Season well and mix all together with water and one fourth teaspoon of Armour's Extract of Beef. Pour into a deep plate, smooth it over and make indentations in the top large enough to hold an egg. Put into the oven until thoroughly heated, and break an egg into each of the places. Return to oven until the eggs are cooked.—E. R. MOTT, PASCOAG, R. I.

HAM CROQUETTES

One cup of finely chopped Armour's Star Ham (cooked), one cup of bread crumbs, two of hot mashed potatoes, one large tablespoon of butter, three eggs, a dash of cayenne. Beat the ham, seasoning and two of the eggs into the potatoes. Let the mixture cool slightly and shape into croquettes. Roll in bread crumbs, dip in beaten egg and again in crumbs. Put into frying basket and plunge into boiling Simon Pure Leaf Lard. Cook two minutes, drain and serve.—MRS. E. A. BERENDSEN, GREEN BAY, WIS.

STUFFED CABBAGE

One medium cabbage, two ounces of Armour's Star Ham, two tablespoons of Armour's Simon Pure Leaf Lard, two egg yolks, one teaspoon each of salt, chopped parsley, and chopped onions, one cup of stale bread crumbs, a dash of cayenne, one pimento pepper chopped. Parboil cabbage, drain and let cool. Open the leaves and scoop out the center. Beat the eggs, add bread moistened with melted Simon Pure Leaf Lard, add the ham and seasoning and all other ingredients. Fill the center, tie cabbage in cheese cloth and boil until tender.—MRS. S. M. FUEICH, JR., 1524 BURDETTE, NEW ORLEANS.

VEAL AND HAM PIE

Cut one and one half pounds of veal into thin slices, also one pound of Armour's Star Ham. Season the veal highly with pepper and salt, with which cover the bottom of roaster. Lay upon this a few slices of ham, then the remainder of the veal and finish with the ham. Add one pint of water in which one teaspoon of Armour's Extract of Beef has been dissolved. Bake one hour. Thirty minutes before serving cover with good paste and bake.—MRS. WARREN YOUNG, LOVELADY, TEXAS.

HAM SALAD

One cup of Armour's Star Ham, one third cup of French peas drained from their liquor, one third cup of celery, one third cup of English walnuts or hickory nuts, one pimento, two small sweet pickles, one hard boiled egg. Chop all ingredients separately and just before serving, mix with a good mayonnaise dressing.—MRS. A. E. RICE, RUSSELLVILLE, KY.

Baking Day

"Baking the way into a man's heart" is a way which has proved successful more than once. But a girl who tried it would be badly handicapped if she did not use the best of materials for the work. Armour's Simon Pure Leaf Lard is the perfect shortening for all kinds of baking.

TEA BISCUITS

Five heaping kitchenspoonfuls of flour and two of sugar, two heaping teaspoonfuls of baking powder. Sift these three times. Add one level tablespoon of Armour's Simon Pure Leaf Lard, rub in well and mix with one egg well beaten, and enough cream or milk to make three fourths of a teacup. Roll out and bake in quick oven. —B. B. BENNETT, 106 WEST NORTH AVE., BALTIMORE, MD.

QUICK CINNAMON ROLLS

One quart of flour, three cups of milk, four tablespoons of Armour's Simon Pure Leaf Lard, two teaspoons of baking powder, one teaspoon of salt. Sift salt and baking powder with flour, chop in the lard, add milk and mix to a soft dough. Roll out in a thin sheet, sprinkle with sugar and cinnamon, add bits of butter and raisins or currants. Roll up as for jelly roll and cut into pieces about half an inch thick. Place in pan and bake. —MISS C. P. LYNCH, 701 JAMES BLDG., CHATTANOOGA.

SPANISH BUN CAKE

One third cup of Armour's Simon Pure Leaf Lard and one third cup of butterine, two cups of white sugar, the yolks of four eggs, one cup of cold water, two heaping cups of flour sifted with two teaspoons of baking powder, one cup each of raisins and nuts. Fold in the whites of four eggs beaten to a stiff froth. Add two teaspoons of ground cinnamon. Ice with caramel icing.—MISS SOPHIA GORDON, COLUMBIA, MO.

RAISIN BREAD

To one cup of bread sponge add one cup of sugar, one cup of raisins, one half cup of Armour's Simon Pure Leaf Lard. Sift one cup of flour with one level teaspoon of soda and a level teaspoon of cloves, cinnamon and allspice. Add to the first mixture with two well-beaten eggs, and beat all until smooth. Bake in a buttered pan in moderate oven.—MISS MAY STONE, UNDERWOOD, MINN.

NUT BREAD

One egg, one half cup of brown sugar, one teaspoon of salt, two cups of milk or water, two tablespoons of Armour's Simon Pure Leaf Lard, four teaspoons of baking powder sifted in four cups of flour, one cup of broken nut meats. Beat well and stand twenty minutes to rise. Bake forty-five minutes to one hour.—CARRIE W. LAMB, 358 WEST 52ND ST., SEATTLE, WASH.

MOTHER'S CAKE

Two cups of sugar, three eggs, one half cup of Armour's Simon Pure Leaf Lard, three cups of flour, three teaspoons of baking powder, one half teaspoon of vanilla extract.

ICING: One generous cup of XXX sugar, softened with a glass of pineapple marmalade and a few drops of vanilla.—MRS. LLOYD R. SHUMAN, THOMPSONTOWN, PA.

CARAMEL PIE

Take the yolks of four eggs, one cup of sugar, four level tablespoons of flour and beat lightly together. Add one pint of sweet milk, put into a double boiler and boil until thick. Then put one cup of sugar into an iron skillet. When melted to a brown syrup pour into the first mixture, adding two tablespoons of melted butter, two teaspoons of vanilla, and bake in a single crust made with two cups of flour, one cup of Armour's Simon Pure Leaf Lard, one half cup of water and a pinch of salt.—MRS. C. A. DOUGLAS, HUMBOLDT, TENN.

GRANDMOTHER'S COOKIES

One cup of sugar, one half cup of Armour's Simon Pure Leaf Lard, one half teaspoon of salt, one egg well beaten, two cups of flour in which two teaspoons of baking powder have been mixed, one cup of sweet milk and one teaspoon of lemon extract. Roll the dough, cut with biscuit cutter and bake in moderate oven.—MISS STELLA SEIROSER, WALTON, KY.

BROWN COOKIES

Boil together for five minutes the following ingredients: One cup of brown sugar, one cup of water, one cup of seeded raisins, one half cup of Armour's Simon Pure Leaf Lard, one teaspoon of ground cinnamon, one half teaspoon of nutmeg and a pinch of salt. Remove from the stove and let cool. When cold add one level teaspoon of soda dissolved in hot water and add three and one half cups of flour and one teaspoon of baking powder. Drop from teaspoon on greased pan and bake in moderate oven.—MRS. EMMETT DAVISON, WOODWARD, OKLA.

WHIPPED CREAM CAKE

Cream together two tablespoons of Armour's Simon Pure Leaf Lard and one cup of sugar. Add a well-beaten egg and half cup of milk. Stir in two and one fourth cups of sifted flour to which have been added two teaspoons of baking powder, and vanilla. Bake in layers in moderate oven about fifteen minutes. When ready to serve, whip one half pint of cream, add two teaspoons of sugar and a little vanilla. Spread between layers and on top layer. Serve on dessert plate with fork.—MRS. WALDO BOGLE, 567 EAST 35TH ST., PORTLAND, OREGON.

RAISIN PIE

Three fourths cup of stoned raisins washed and chopped, one fourth cup of currants washed and chopped, pinch of salt, one tablespoon of vinegar, two tablespoons of butter, one half cup of molasses, one cup of brown sugar, two cups of water. Thoroughly mix the above and boil together for ten minutes, then thicken with five tablespoons of flour mixed with water. For the crust take one heaping cup of flour, one half teaspoon of salt, one half teaspoon of baking powder, one third cup of Armour's Simon Pure Leaf Lard, and enough cold water to make a stiff dough.—MRS. MABEL G. WARNER, 27 PEYTON ST., SANTA CRUZ, CALIF.

FRUIT CAKE FROM BREAD DOUGH

Rub together until creamy one half cup of butter or Glendale Butterine, one half cup of Armour's Simon Pure Leaf Lard and two cups of granulated sugar. Add three eggs well beaten, one cup of raisins, one teaspoon of cinnamon, one teaspoon of nutmeg, one half teaspoon of soda dissolved in a little water. Add this mixture to three cups of very light sponge and beat well, adding a little more flour if needed. Should be as thick as ordinary loaf cake batter. Fill greased bread pans half full and let rise one hour. Bake in a moderate oven forty-five minutes.—MRS. M. L. CURZON, 845 PENNSYLVANIA AVENUE, MILWAUKEE, WIS.

WINE DROPS

Two eggs, two cups of sugar, one cup of molasses, three fourths cup of coffee, one small teaspoon of salt, five large tablespoons of Armour's Simon Pure Leaf Lard melted, two teaspoons of soda dissolved in the coffee, one teaspoon of cloves and one of cinnamon, one cup of raisins and five cups of flour. Drop by spoonfuls on buttered tins and bake in quick oven.—MRS. E. W. PINE, CLARESHOLM, ALBERTA, CANADA.

The Daily Menu

Planning the days meals ahead is a big help in systematizing the days work. The following menus—each of which has won a prize of FIVE DOLLARS—show how women in all states of the union have planned nourishing, economical meals.

ALABAMA

MRS. A. M. CRUM, 622 MORRISON AVE., FLORENCE

BREAKFAST—Soft Peaches halved with whipped Cream, Oatmeal and Cream, French Fried Potatoes, Corn Bread Sticks, Broiled Star Ham with Cream Gravy, Soft Boiled Eggs, Hot Biscuit, Butter, Coffee.

LUNCHEON—Veribest Tomato Soup, Bread Toasted in Small Squares, Creamed Potatoes with Shredded Star Ham and Mayonnaise Dressing, Tomatoes Stuffed with Chopped Celery, Sliced Sweet Potatoes with Cream Dressing, Strawberry Jello with Whipped Cream, Marshmallow Cake and Iced Tea.

DINNER—Spiced Star Ham Boiled, Veribest Pork and Beans, Rice Cakes Fried, Creamed Potatoes, Corn Pudding, Tomatoes Stuffed with Salad made of Veribest Potted Ham, Pineapple Cake, Sherbet, Coffee.

ARIZONA

MERTIE R. JONES, MESA

BREAKFAST—Cereal with Cream and Sugar, Broiled Star Bacon, Poached Eggs, Graham Gems, Coffee.

43

LUNCHEON—Chicken Bouillon (Armour's Bouillon Cubes), Creamed Veribest Chicken in Biscuit Cases, French Fried Potatoes (Fried in Simon Pure Leaf Lard), Brown Bread and Butterine Sandwiches (Armour's Glendale Butterine), Cake, Armour's Grape Juice, Iced.

DINNER—Cream of Veribest Tomato Soup, Veribest Roast Beef with Brown Sauce (Made from Armour's Extract of Beef), Veribest Pork and Beans, Potatoes, Creamed Onions, Armour's Grape Juice Ice, Small Cakes, Coffee.

ARKANSAS

MRS. W. H. BLAKELY, 713 NORTH 19TH ST., FORT SMITH

BREAKFAST—Oranges, Armour's Star Bacon Broiled, Poached Eggs, Toast, Coffee.

LUNCHEON—Sliced Veribest Tongue, Hashed Browned Potatoes, Rolls, Individual Custards in Ramekins, Tea.

DINNER—Cream Tomato Soup (Veribest), Casserole Roast (Veribest Roast Beef), Candied Sweet Potatoes, Stuffed Green Peppers (Filling of Bread Crumbs, Onion, Veribest Deviled Ham), Pineapple and Cheese Salad on Lettuce, Mayonnaise Dressing, Potato Rolls, Frozen Apricots in Tall Glasses of Whipped Cream, Angel Food Cake, Coffee.

CALIFORNIA

MRS. EDITH V. SCHLIEMANN, SUSANVILLE

BREAKFAST—Corn Flakes, Broiled Star Ham, Poached Eggs, Fried Potatoes, Toast, Chocolate.

LUNCHEON—Veribest Pork and Beans, Egg Salad, Hot Biscuits, Raspberry Shortcake, Armour's Grape Juice Lemonade.

DINNER—Veribest Consomme, Rice Curry and Veribest Veal, Creamed Peas, French Fried Potatoes, Lettuce Salad, Plum Cake, Iced Tea.

COLORADO

MRS. BURTON A. SMEAD, 1281 SOUTH DOWNING ST., DENVER

BREAKFAST—Rolled Oats with Hot Dates, Liver and Star Bacon Skewered and Broiled, Popovers, Coffee.

LUNCHEON—Creamed Veribest Chicken in Pastry Shells, French Fried Sweet Potatoes, Bread and Butter, Orange Marmalade, Tea.

DINNER—Mock Turtle Soup (Armour's Extract of Beef), Croutons, Two-inch Slice of Star Ham Braised with Tomato Sauce, Boiled Rice, Green String Beans, Jellied Celery Relish (Armour's Beef Bouillon Cubes), Bread, Snow Pudding, Sponge Cake, Coffee.

CONNECTICUT

P. CURTIN, EDSON HOUSE, PLANTSVILLE

BREAKFAST—Fruit, Buckwheat Cakes with Armour's Star Bacon, Rolls, Coffee.

DINNER—Armour's Star Ham Soup, Veribest Roast Beef with Brown Sauce, Baked Potatoes, Creamed Onions, Veribest Mince Meat Pie, Coffee.

SUPPER—Armour's Veribest Pork and Beans, Brown Bread, Armour's Hot Chicken Bouillon with Butter Thins.

DELAWARE

MRS. G. A. SMITH, EDGEMOORE, ROUTE 2, BOX 81A.

BREAKFAST—Grapefruit, Star Ham Omelet, Tomato Catsup, Hot Cakes, Coffee.

LUNCHEON—Cream of Onion Soup, Little Pigs in Blankets (Armour's Star Bacon), Tomato Catsup, French Fried Potatoes, Iced Tea, Peach Shortcake.

DINNER—Veribest Veal Loaf, Riced Potatoes, Tomatoes Stuffed with Star Ham, Hot Rolls, Grape Sherbet (Armour's Grape Juice).

DISTRICT OF COLUMBIA

MRS. E. W. SILLINGS, 625 E. St. S. E., Washington

BREAKFAST—Grapefruit with Armour's Grape Juice, Star Ham Croquettes, Baked Potatoes, Buttered Toast, Cocoa.

LUNCHEON—Veribest Boned Chicken, Sweet Potatoes, Gravy, Apple Sauce, White Bread, Cookies, Milk Shake.

DINNER—Split Pea Soup with Crackers, Roast Star Ham with Parsnips, Stuffed Cabbage, Sliced Tomatoes, Brown Bread, Peach Short Cake, Iced Postum.

FLORIDA

IDA C. WESTGAARD, Buena Vista, Dade Co.

BREAKFAST—Iced Grapes, Puffed Rice with Cream, Broiled Star Bacon, Poached Eggs on Toast, Coffee.

LUNCHEON—Veribest Tomato Soup, Boiled Potatoes with Cream Sauce, Cold Baked Star Ham Sliced, Bread and Butter, Hot Gingerbread, Jelly, Coffee.

DINNER—Bouillon (Armour's Bouillon Cubes), Veribest Roast Beef with Mushroom Sauce, Creamed Asparagus, Candied Sweet Potatoes, Tomato Jelly, Salad with Mayonnaise, Armour's Grape Juice Sherbet, Cake, Coffee Mints.

GEORGIA

MRS. NELLIE H. DUSENBURY, 997 Milledge Ave., Athens

BREAKFAST—Figs with Cream, Creamed Chipped Beef (Veribest), Saratoga Chips, Sliced Tomatoes, Hot Rolls, Tea, Coffee.

LUNCHEON—Stuffed Peppers (Force Meat made from Veribest Veal Loaf), Light Bread, Veribest Pork and Beans, Pickled Beets, Armour's Grape Juice Frappe, Angel Food Cake, Iced Tea.

DINNER—Fruit Cocktail, Tomato Soup (Seasoned with Armour's Extract of Beef), Baked Star Ham, Creamed Onions, Squash, Tomato and Asparagus Salad with French Dressing, Bread Sticks, Fresh Peaches with Cream, Coffee with Cheese Wafers.

IDAHO

MRS. H. W. ZIMMERMAN, PAYETTE

BREAKFAST—Cantaloupe, Fried Star Bacon and Eggs, Toast with White Sauce, Oatmeal Cookies, Coffee.

LUNCHEON—Veribest Pork and Beans, Hot Rolls and Honey, Sliced Tomatoes, Potato Chips, Baked Apple with Cream Sauce, Iced Tea.

DINNER—Veribest Tomato Soup, Veribest Creamed Chicken, Baked Potatoes, Cabbage Salad, Carrots and Peas, Peaches and Cream, Cake, Coffee.

ILLINOIS

ELIZABETH M. VAN HUYSEN, 501 CEDAR ST., QUINCY

BREAKFAST—Green Gage Plums, Cereal and Cream, Armour's Star Bacon and Fried Eggs, Simon Pure Parker House Rolls, New White Clover Honey, Coffee.

LUNCHEON—Veribest Pork and Beans, Brown Bread and Butter Sandwiches, Tomato Salad, Simon Pure Doughnuts, Armour's Grape Juice.

DINNER—Veribest Tomato Soup with Croutons, Veribest Roast Beef with Browned Sweet Potatoes, Green Corn on Cob, Beet Salad, Mashed Potatoes, Simon Pure Concord Grape Pie, Coffee, Cheese Wafers.

INDIANA

MRS. L. B. KILMER, BURDICK

BREAKFAST—Apple Fritters or Baked Apples, Star Ham Rolls, Soft Boiled Eggs, Corn Meal Mush (Fried in Simon Pure Leaf Lard), Coffee, Hot Milk.

LUNCHEON—Hot Beef Bouillon (Armour's Bouillon Cubes), Cheese Sticks, Armour's Veribest Beef Tongue and Tomato Salad, Cream Biscuits, Apple Sauce, Grape Juice with Marshmallows.

DINNER—Veribest Soup, Ragout of Beef (Armour's Veribest), Potatoes and Brown Gravy flavored with Beef Extract, Escalloped Tomatoes, Cream of Grape Pie (Made with Armour's Grape Juice and Simon Pure Leaf Lard), Coffee.

IOWA

MRS. J. C. BRANDT, LE MARS

BREAKFAST—Chilled White Grapes in Cantaloupe, Corn Meal and Ham Mush (Fried in Bacon Grease), Broiled Star Bacon, Toast with Honey, Doughnuts and Coffee.

LUNCHEON—Veribest Corned Beef au Gratin, Graham and White Bread Sandwiches, Rhubarb Marmalade, Cheese, Simon Pure Leaf Lard Cake, Sliced Peaches, Armour's Mulled Grape Juice.

DINNER—Bouillon (Armour's Bouillon Cubes), Croutons, Casserole of Veal, Riced Potatoes, Armour's Baked Beans, Stuffed Tomatoes,

Veribest Tongue and Egg Salad, White Bread (Butterine in balls and sprig of parsley), Armour's Mince Meat Pie, Coffee.

KANSAS

MRS. J. L. HOBBS, 309 WABASH AVE., WICHITA

BREAKFAST—Iced Cantaloupe, Shredded Wheat Biscuits with Sugar and Cream, Veribest Corned Beef Hash, Baking Powder Biscuits, Apple Butter, Coffee.

LUNCHEON—Star Ham Souffle, Creamed Potatoes, Fresh Rolls, Blackberry Jam, Tea.

DINNER—Veribest Tomato Soup with Toast Cubes, Veribest Roast Beef with Potatoes and Brown Gravy, Creamed Cauliflower, Veribest Chicken Salad served in Red Pepper Shells on Lettuce Leaves, Cheese Sandwiches, Olives, Banana Shortcake with Whipped Cream, Coffee.

KENTUCKY

MRS. M. GEO. MOORE, R. 5, LEXINGTON

BREAKFAST—Bananas with Cereal and Cream, Broiled Star Bacon, Fried Apples, Creamed Hominy, Buttermilk Biscuit, Blackberry Jam, Coffee.

LUNCHEON—Cream of (Veribest) Tomato Soup, Sweet Peppers stuffed with Veribest Veal Loaf, Escalloped Corn, Cottage Cheese with Cream, Sally Lunn, Tea.

DINNER—Bouillon (Armour's Bouillon Cubes), Baked Star Ham, Corn Pudding, Sweet Potatoes, Green Beans, Tomatoes with Mayonnaise Dressing, Veribest Chicken Salad, Amber Pie (Simon Pure Leaf Lard), Cheese, Coffee.

LOUISIANA

MRS. T. J. BINGHAM, CONCORDIA PARISH, VIDALIA

BREAKFAST—Broiled Star Ham, Poached Eggs on Toast, Hot Muffins, Butter, Coffee.

LUNCHEON—Chicken Bouillon (Armour's Bouillon Cubes), Veribest Veal Loaf, Raisin Bread, Butter, Cream Puffs (Made of Simon Pure Leaf Lard), Iced Armour's Grape Juice.

DINNER—Cream of Corn Soup, Broiled Chicken on Toast with Baked Apples, Stuffed Peppers (Using Armour's Star Ham Minced), Scalloped Potatoes, Fruit Salad with Mayonnaise, Mince Meat Pie with Hard Sauce (Veribest Mince Meat), Coffee, Mints.

MAINE

MISS GERTRUDE JONES, 59 COTTAGE ST., SO. PORTLAND

BREAKFAST—Bananas and Cream, Star Ham Omelet, Rye Biscuit, Breakfast Cake, Coffee.

LUNCHEON—Veribest Vegetable Soup, Simon Pure Luncheon Rolls, Creamed Potatoes, Orange Sauce, Iced Tea.

SUPPER—Stuffed Baked Ham, Irish Potatoes, Baked Onions, Armour's Grape Juice Sherbet, Cake, Coffee.

MARYLAND

MRS. GEO. E. LOANE, 711 E. 22ND ST., BALTIMORE

BREAKFAST—Oranges, Grapenuts with Cream, Armour's Star Bacon, Bread dipped in Egg and fried in Bacon Fat or Simon Pure Leaf Lard, Corn Pone, Cloverbloom Butter, Coffee.

DINNER—Armour's Veribest Tomato Soup, Croquettes of Veribest Chicken, Mashed Potatoes, Lima Beans with Cream Dressing, Lettuce Salad, Ice Cream and Black Coffee.

SUPPER—Slice Boiled Star Ham, Tomato Salad, Biscuit, Cheese, Cake, Tea.

MASSACHUSETTS

MISS ISABELLE M. WALKER, 17 Hovey Ave., Cambridge

BREAKFAST—Cracked Wheat, Corn Bread, Star Ham Omelet, Coffee.

LUNCHEON—Extract of Beef, Croutons, Apple Turnovers, Russian Tea.

DINNER—Veribest Roast Beef, Baked Sweet Potatoes, Pickled Beets, Boiled Rice, Syrup, Tea.

MICHIGAN

MRS. THOS. WESTWOOD, 2309 S. Mich. Ave., Saginaw, W. S.

BREAKFAST—Wheatena with Dates, Sugar and Cream, French Toast, Broiled Star Ham, Golden Omelet, Peach Marmalade, Fried Cakes, Coffee.

DINNER—Noodle Soup (Armour's Extract of Beef), Creamed Chicken (Armour's Veribest) in Riced Potato Border, Ginger Pears, Watermelon Pickles, Beet and Tomato Salad, Strawberry Custard, Grape Juice Moussé, Coffee, Black Tea.

SUPPER—English Tea Cakes, Fruit Salad, Veribest Tongue Garnished with Shoe String Potatoes, Peanut Cookies, Cocoa with Whipped Cream.

MINNESOTA

LILLIAN HUDSON, 1809 FREMONT AVE. SO. MINNEAPOLIS

BREAKFAST—Oranges, Boiled Star Ham, Oatmeal with Sugar and Cream, Creamed Potatoes, Popovers, Coffee.

LUNCHEON—Cold Sliced Armour's Star Ham, Cheese Fondue, Bread and Butter, Sliced Peaches, Cookies, Coffee.

DINNER—Tomato Soup, Braised Beef, Riced Potatoes, Squash, Refugee Stringless Bean Salad, Baking Powder Biscuits (Armour's Simon Pure Leaf Lard), Cherry Pie, Coffee.

MISSISSIPPI

MISS LOLA PERRY, 912 39TH AVE., MERIDIAN

BREAKFAST—Baked Bananas, Creamed Veribest Corned Beef, Potato Chips, French Toast, Coffee.

LUNCHEON—Veribest Ox Tail Soup, Armour Star Ham Timbales, Deviled Eggs, Jellied Baked Apples, Parker House Rolls, Iced Tea.

DINNER—Fricassee of Veribest Roast Beef, Creamed Cauliflower, Shrimp Salad, Spaghetti with Tomato Sauce, Philadelphia Potatoes, Angel Cake, Grape Nectar (Armour's Grape Juice).

MISSOURI

MISS SOPHIA GORDON, R. 1, COLUMBIA

BREAKFAST—Peaches and Cream, Broiled Star Bacon, Eggs on Toast, Graham Cakes with Maple Syrup, Coffee.

LUNCHEON—Tomato Soup Served with Whipped Cream, Crackers, Fish Croquettes with Sliced Lemon, Apple and Nut Salad, Baked Sweet Peppers with Tabasco Sauce, Light Rolls, Iced Tea.

DINNER—Cold Boiled Star Ham, Asparagus on Toast, French Fried Potatoes, Sliced Tomatoes, Hot Biscuits, Armour's Grape Ice, Cake, Coffee, Mints.

MONTANA

MRS. GEO. SINCLAIR, 130 GRANDE AVE., BILLINGS

BREAKFAST—Sliced Peaches, Cereal, Star Ham and Eggs, Toast, Coffee.

LUNCHEON—Veribest Veal Loaf with White Sauce, Sliced Tomatoes, One Egg Muffins, Cantaloupe with Ice Cream, Iced Tea, Wafers.

DINNER—Fried Chicken with Extract of Beef Sauce, Riced Potatoes, Green Corn on the Cob, Rolls, Olives and Sweet Midgets, Stewed Pears, Sponge Cake, Tea.

NEBRASKA

MRS. DAISY CANNON, BURTON

BREAKFAST—Oranges (Halved), Puffed Rice with Sugar and Cream, Star Ham and Eggs (Baked), Hot Breakfast Rolls, Strawberry Jam, Graham Wafers, Coffee.

LUNCHEON—Fruit Salad, Chicken Bouillon (Armour's), Sliced Cold Star Ham, Mashed Potatoes with Border of Buttered Peas, Sliced Tomatoes, Buns, Simon Pure Marshmallow Delights, Ice Cream with Nuts, Armour's Grape Juice.

DINNER—Veribest Vegetable Soup, Beef en Casserole, Creamed Cabbage, Veribest Bean Croquettes with Cubes of Tomato Jelly, Cold Mashed Potato Balls, Peas, Onions with Salad Dressing, Graham and White Bread, Salted Cherries, Nuts, Fruit Cake (Made with Veribest Mince Meat), Grape Juice (Armour's), Charlotte Russe, Coffee.

NEVADA

MRS. C. E. CADY, Montello

BREAKFAST—Puffed Wheat, Sliced Apples and Cream, Armour's Star Ham and Eggs Fried, Fried Sweet Potatoes, Young Onions, Hot Cinnamon Rolls, Buttered Toast, Coffee.

LUNCHEON—Combination Salad, Bouillon (Armour's Bouillon Cubes), Armour's Veribest Deviled Tongue, Sliced Cold, Veribest Pork and Beans, Cantaloupe a la Mode, White Bread, Iced Tea.

DINNER—Veribest Vegetable Soup, Watercress Salad, Spiced Veribest Roast Beef, Cold Boiled Star Ham, Stewed Carrots, Escalloped Onions, Baked Potatoes, Hot Biscuits, Blanc Mange, Apple Pie with Cheese, Milk.

NEW HAMPSHIRE

MRS. ALMOND SMITH, New London

BREAKFAST—Peaches and Cream, Puffed Rice and Cream, Star Bacon and Eggs, Creamed Potatoes, Popovers, Coffee.

DINNER—Veribest Chicken Soup with Bread Sticks, Tomato and Cucumber Salad, Veribest Roast Beef with Brown Gravy, Mashed Potatoes, Sweet Potatoes Boiled, Sweet Corn, Apple Tapioca Pudding, Grape Juice and Crackers.

SUPPER—Creamed Veribest Chicken, Baking Powder Biscuits, Pickled Beets, Cranberry Tarts, Mocha Cake, Tea.

NEW JERSEY

MRS. WM. H. REGER, White House Sta.

BREAKFAST—Baked Apples, Graham Mush, Eggs Shirred on Mince of Veribest Veal, Simon Pure Hasty Biscuit, Coffee.

LUNCHEON—Veribest Chicken Salad Sandwiches, Fried Oysters (Simon Pure Leaf Lard), Peach Shortcake, Armour's Grape Juice.

DINNER—Chicken Bouillon (Armour's), Braised Beef Heart, Mashed Potatoes, Macaroni, Spinach Timbales, String Bean Salad, Cocoanut Pie.

NEW MEXICO

MRS. D. E. BREWER, COLUMBUS, BOX 136

BREAKFAST—Fruit, Star Ham, Eggs, Hot Cakes, Doughnuts, Coffee.

LUNCHEON—Musk Melon, Spiced Ham, Egg Salad, Bread and Butter Sandwiches, Marshmallow Cake, Tea.

DINNER—French Peas and Chicken, Veribest Roast Veal, Brown Potatoes, Tomato Relish, Baked Greens, Waldorf Salad, Washington Pie, Coffee.

NEW YORK

MRS. ELEANOR EVERTS, 66 EAGLE ST., FREDONIA

BREAKFAST—Sliced Peaches, Cream of Wheat, Broiled Star Ham, Baked Potatoes, Graham Gems, Ginger Cookies, Coffee.

LUNCHEON—Veribest Beef Loaf, Fresh Rolls, Glendale Butterine, Pear Conserve, Apple Pie, Cheese, Armour's Grape Juice.

DINNER—Veribest Tomato Soup, Saltines, Veal Pocket (Extract of Beef), Mashed Potatoes, Brown Gravy, Green Corn Pudding, Red Cabbage Salad, Salt Rising Bread, Blackberry Pudding, Pumpkin Pie, Coffee.

NORTH CAROLINA

MRS. WM. H. BOND, 435 CUTLER ST., BOYLAN HEIGHTS, RALEIGH

BREAKFAST—Fresh Figs and Cream, Poached Eggs on Toast, Star Brand Bacon Panned, One-Egg Muffins, Coffee.

LUNCHEON—Veribest Veal Loaf with White Sauce and Pimentos, Perfection Salad, Swedish Rolls, Sliced Peaches and Cream, Tea.

DINNER—Veribest Ox Tail Soup, Escalloped Chicken, Baked Bananas, Asparagus Vinagrette, Potatoes au Gratin, Stuffed Cucumbers, Pineapple Short Cake with Whipped Cream, Coffee, Toasted Crackers and Cheese.

NORTH DAKOTA

MRS. T. J. TIDEMANSON, WYNDMERE

BREAKFAST—Grapefruit, Armour's Star Bacon and Eggs, Muffins, Coffee.

LUNCHEON—Veribest Veal Loaf, Celery and Apple Salad, Corn Bread, Maple Syrup, Tea.

DINNER—Veribest Tomato Bouillon, Armour's Star Ham Baked, Creamed Potatoes, Creamed Onions, Lettuce Salad, Apple Pie.

OHIO

MRS. E. WIEMEYER, 2860 COLERAIN AVE., CINCINNATI

BREAKFAST—Corn Fritters, Apple Sauce, Fried Star Ham and Eggs, Currant Bread, Coffee.

LUNCHEON—Roast Beef Pie, Fried Sweet Potatoes, Stuffed Tomatoes, Soda Wafers, Tomato Bouillon, Grape Jelly.

DINNER—Brunswick Stew made from Veribest Beef and Chicken, Lyonnaise Potatoes, Sliced Tomatoes, Custard Junket, Coffee.

OKLAHOMA

MRS. E. ANDREWS, 625 W. 18TH ST., OKLAHOMA CITY

BREAKFAST—Grapefruit with Armour's Grape Juice, Cereal, Star Ham, Poached Eggs, Biscuits, Coffee.

LUNCHEON—Bouillon (Armour's Bouillon Cubes), Veribest Creamed Chicken, Stuffed Tomatoes, Rolls, Hot Tea.

DINNER—Veribest Vegetable Soup, Baked Star Ham, Baked Sweet Potatoes, Escalloped Corn, Combination Salad, Apple Dumplings, Coffee.

OREGON

MRS. DAN FISHER, BROWNSVILLE

BREAKFAST—Cracked Wheat Mush with Dates, Mountain Trout with Star Bacon, Potato Chips, Strawberry Jam, Popovers, Coffee.

DINNER—Chicken Bouillon (Armour's Bouillon Cubes), Served with Popped Corn, Baked Ham in Cider, Fried Apples, Banana and Peanut Salad, Browned Potatoes, Pineapple Cream Pie.

SUPPER—Veal Loaf (Veribest), Tomatoes Stuffed with Corn, Wilted Lettuce, Rye Bread, Cantaloupe filled with Grape Sherbet.

PENNSYLVANIA

MRS. H. C. WEINSTOCK, 5410 GIRARD AVE., PHILADELPHIA

BREAKFAST—Sliced Bananas and Corn Flakes with Sugar and Cream. Veribest Sausage on Simon Pure Waffles, Rolls, Butter, Cocoa, Coffee.

LUNCHEON—Veribest Tomato Soup with Croutons, Club Sandwiches (Veribest Chicken and Star Bacon), Creamed Potatoes, Cakes, Fruit, Tea.

DINNER—Grape Fruit Salad, Beef Bouillon (Armour's Bouillon Cubes), Baked Star Ham (Baked and Served with Champagne Sauce), Asparagus on Toast, Mashed Sweet Potatoes, Sliced Tomatoes and Lettuce, French Dressing (Simon Pure), Peach Dumplings, Whole Wheat Crackers and Cheese, Coffee, Mints.

RHODE ISLAND

MAUDE E. SEARS, 10 VERNDALE AVE., PROVIDENCE

BREAKFAST—Bananas, Hominy with Cream, Star Ham with Fried Eggs, French Fried Potatoes, Toast, Coffee.

LUNCHEON—Beef Bouillon (Armour's Bouillon Cubes), Sliced Tongue with Tomato Sauce, Cream of Tartar Biscuits, Sliced Peaches, Honey Gingerbread, Armour's Grape Juice.

DINNER—Veribest Tomato Soup, Milk Crackers, Veribest Creamed Chicken en Casserole, Baked Potatoes, Apple Fritters, Stewed Tomatoes, Celery, Ambrosia, Sponge Cake, Coffee.

SOUTH CAROLINA

MRS. S. E. TRUE, 108 ST. JOHN ST., SPARTANBURG

BREAKFAST—Iced Cantaloupe, Cereal and Cream Poached Eggs on Toast Garnished with Crisp Star Bacon, Waffles and Maple Syrup, Coffee.

DINNER—Veribest Tomato Bouillon, Wafers, Broiled Trout with Mashed Potatoes, Star Boiled Ham Sliced Thin, Peas in Timbales, Macaroni au Gratin, Rolls, Sliced Tomatoes on Lettuce with Mayonnaise Dressing, Caramel Ice Cream, Cake, Coffee.

SUPPER—Veribest Chicken Sandwiches, Celery and Nut Salad, Salted Crackers, Armour's Grape Juice Sherbet, Oatmeal Cakes, Iced Tea.

SOUTH DAKOTA

MRS. WALTER YORKER, BOX 471, BERESFORD

BREAKFAST—Sliced Peaches, Creamed Veribest Dried Beef, Bran Muffins, Raisin Cookies, Coffee.

LUNCHEON—Veribest Baked Beans, Apple Sauce, Rye Bread, Angel Food Cake, Cocoa.

DINNER—Veribest Tomato Soup, Veribest Roast Beef with Cream Gravy, Baked Sweet Potatoes, Pickled Pears, Rolls, Cream Pie, Coffee, After Dinner Mints.

TENNESSEE

MISS ROBERTA FRY, R. F. D. NO. 10, COLUMBIA

BREAKFAST—Grapefruit, Cream of Wheat, Star Bacon, Eggs, Hot Biscuits, Blackberry Jelly, Coffee.

LUNCHEON—Veribest Creamed Chicken, Tomato and Green Pepper Salad, Bread and Butter Sandwiches, Applesauce, Doughnuts, Iced Tea.

DINNER—-Veribest Tomato Soup, Mashed Potatoes, Veribest Pork and Beans, Baked Star Ham, Creamed Peas, Hot Rolls, Sweet Pickles, Armour's Grape Juice Sherbet, Cake, Coffee.

TEXAS

MRS. M. E. SCOVILL, KENEDY

BREAKFAST—Fruit, Oatmeal with Sugar and Cream, Frizzled Star Ham and Eggs, Delmonico Potatoes, Raised Biscuits, Coffee.

LUNCHEON—Cream of Tomato Soup (Veribest), Veribest Beef Loaf, Tomato Salad, Rye Bread, Butter, Nut Cake, Armour's Grape Juice Punch.

DINNER—Armour's Bouillon, Roast Loin of Pork, Apple Sauce, Rice, Creamed Turnips, Celery Mayonnaise, Wafers, Cheese, Armour's Mince Meat Tarts, Coffee.

UTAH

MRS. EMMA CALDWELL, MURRAY

BREAKFAST—Sliced Peaches, Grape-Nuts and Cream, Star Ham fried, Poached Eggs on Toast, Graham Gems, Grapes, Postum.

LUNCHEON—Veribest Cold Tongue, Homemade Mustard Pickles, Sliced Tomatoes, Luncheon Rolls, Peach Sherbet, Feather Cake, Ice Tea.

DINNER—Veribest Tomato Soup, Crackers, Veribest Chicken Creamed, Mashed Potatoes, Browned Cabbage, String Beans, Cream Cocoanut Pie, Watermelon, Coffee.

VERMONT

MRS. HENRY J. McNALLY, 91 CHERRY ST., BURLINGTON

BREAKFAST—Peaches and Cream, Broiled Star Ham, Creamed Potatoes, Poached Eggs, Triscuit, Graham Muffins and Postum.

LUNCHEON—Armour's Beef Bouillon, Chicken Salad from Veribest Chicken, Brown Bread and Butter Sandwiches, Sunshine Cookies, Armour's Grape Juice.

DINNER—Stuffed Tomatoes on Lettuce Leaves with Mayonnaise Dressing, Veribest Beef Loaf with Brown Sauce flavored with Armour's Extract of Beef, Riced Potatoes, Evergreen Corn on Cobb, Beet Pickles, Bread and Butter, Armour's Grape Juice Frappe, Chocolate Tokens, Coffee.

VIRGINIA

MISS ELSIE A. SHEETZ, 715 E. GRACE ST., RICHMOND

BREAKFAST—Cereal, Fried Apples with Star Bacon, Cornmeal Muffins, Coffee.

DINNER—Bouillon from Armour's Bouillon Cubes, Veribest Chicken Pie, Creamed Peas and Carrots, Potato Salad, Hot Rolls, Date Pudding, Coffee.

SUPPER—Armour's Tomato Soup with Croutons, Veribest Bean and Celery Salad, Cold Sliced Tongue, Hot Biscuits, Jelly, Tea.

WASHINGTON

MISS B. E. SMITH, R. F. D. NO. 36, Burton

BREAKFAST—Iced Cantaloupe, Armour's Fancy Select Eggs fried with Armour's Star Bacon, Corn Muffins, Coffee.

LUNCHEON—Veribest Pork and Beans, Cucumber and Tomato Salad, Devil's Cake, Sliced Peaches, Tea.

DINNER—Veribest Tomato Soup, Veribest Boned Chicken in Bechamel Sauce, French Fried Potatoes, Cauliflower, Blackberry Pie, Cheese, Coffee.

WEST VIRGINIA

MRS. M. L. WHITE, 1409 Magazine St., Charleston

BREAKFAST—Cream of Wheat with Maple Syrup, Fried Star Ham and Eggs, Hot Biscuits and Butter, Coffee.

LUNCHEON—Corn Beef Hash, Baked Apples, Potato Salad, Lettuce, Cream Cake, Tea.

DINNER—Tomato Soup (Veribest), Cream Potatoes, String Bean Salad, Sliced Tomatoes, Pickles, Sliced Star Ham, Hot Rolls, Coffee.

WISCONSIN

MISS GENEVIEVE RAYMOND, Eagle River

BREAKFAST—Cereal with Dates, Broiled Star Bacon, Buttered Toast, Boiled Eggs, Coffee.

LUNCHEON—Veribest Vegetable Soup with Crisp Crackers, Celery, Stewed Figs, Chocolate Marble Cake, Armour's Grape Juice.

DINNER—Veribest Chicken Fricasseed, Mashed Potatoes, Baked Squash, Creamed Turnips, Green Tomato Pickle, Watermelon, Pumpkin Pie, Coffee.

WYOMING

MRS. A. M. HUMPHRY, 646 SUMMER ST., SHERIDAN

BREAKFAST—Graham Porridge with Dates, Fried Star Ham and Eggs, Dry Toast and Butter, Coffee.

LUNCHEON—Veribest Chicken Sandwiches, Creamed Potatoes, Tomato and Lettuce Salad, Hot Doughnuts (Armour's Simon Pure Leaf Lard), Tea.

DINNER—Veribest Vegetable Soup with Croutons, Veribest Roast Beef, Brown Sauce, Browned Potatoes, Cauliflower au Gratin, Rolls, Beet Pickles, Armour's Grape Juice Sherbet, Cake, Nuts, Coffee.

CANADA

MRS. G. E. POSTE, 231 MOSS ST., VICTORIA, B. C.

BREAKFAST—Oranges, Wheat Flakes with Cream, Baked Hash (Veribest Beef), Preserved Peaches, Muffins, Coffee.

DINNER—Veribest Tomato Soup, Baked Stuffed (Star) Ham, Mashed Potatoes, Creamed Cauliflower, Pickled Carrots, Chocolate Pie, Tea.

SUPPER—Sliced Meat Loaf, Potato Salad Garnished with Sliced Hard Boiled Eggs and Parsley, Raspberry Preserve, Cheese, Lemon Tarts, Cake, Cocoa.

Little Stories by Our Readers

A Ham Story

As we are lovers of good ham we always use Armour's Star Brand. I generally buy the ham on Saturday as it keeps better than fresh meat. I buy a whole ham (try to get one about ten pounds), then get the dealer to cut two nice slices thick enough to broil, a little beyond the center, leaving two nice ends, the string end the smaller. One slice I use for Sunday morning Breakfast, the other one I wrap in a moist cloth, place between two plates. This will keep three or four days.

I now take the large end, put it on in cold water, let simmer for a couple of hours, then take out and drain; cut off skin, and part of the fat and put it in the oven to finish cooking. The skin I save for use on the griddle, the fat I render and use the dripping for salads. After baking, serve hot or cold, sliced; I still have a small end and one slice left, the small end I boil until thoroughly done, take out and use the water for vegetables, such as cabbage, spinach, beans, etc. The small end does not slice as well as the other so I take all the meat from the bone, and put it through the chopper, grind it fine, and use it for ham loaf, toast filling for tomato cups or for ham omelet. The baked end I serve sliced, also, use for sandwiches. If I have to keep the sandwiches I put them in a moistened napkin; it keeps the ham moist and juicy.

How I Arrange to Use a Whole Ham

SUNDAY BREAKFAST: Water cress, slice Star Ham broiled with milk gravy, hot rolls, coffee, home-made peach cake.

SUNDAY DINNER: Beef pot roast, white potatoes whipped, sweet potatoes roasted under the meat, cauliflower boiled in the ham water, cream dressing, fruit sherbet, in which I use Armour's Grape Juice.

SUNDAY SUPPER: Cold baked Star Ham sliced thin, or tomato cups on lettuce with mustard dressing, white bread and butter, home-made cake, sliced peaches, and tea.

To make TOMATO CUPS, take medium size tomatoes, skin them (by pouring boiling water over them first, this is easily done) and put on ice until cold; scoop out the center. Make a filling of minced ham, a little chicken, breadcrumbs (equal parts), a seasoning of chopped peppers; fill tomatoes; on top of each put a little mustard dressing. Set each cup on a lettuce leaf, and serve.

Now I still have one slice of ham left, some minced ham, some of the baked ham. The last slice I broil and serve with poached eggs; the baked ham, makes sandwiches. The week I buy a whole ham I don't buy much other meat. Trusting this will be of value to some, I remain,—I. M. B., Philadelphia.

Milk Toast

"Have kept Armour's Beef Extract always on hand for years and it has helped me out of many a tight place. One day the children teased for milk toast for supper, and to my dismay I found the milk was 'short' that day. Not wishing to disappoint them I tried to see what I could do. I made a consommé with Armour's Beef Extract, using a quarter teaspoonful to a cup and seasoning it with salt and pepper, and used this in the same way as I would milk. Our 'milk' toast was fit for a king. The children pronounced it the best ever. In these times of high prices, with milk at ten cents per quart, many a family would welcome such an excellent substitute as Armour's Extract."

Most useful are the Armour's Bouillon Cubes. I use them in preparing soups, gravies, dissolved and poured over a roast while cooking. I give my husband and children each one in a cup of hot water, every morning for breakfast, the first thing, as it seems to be an appetizer; also serve it to my aged parents in the morning before rising, as it gives them strength to make their toilet. They are both very aged and failing and the effect of the bouillon is wonderful. My husband also takes Armour's Bouillon Cubes with him in his lunch basket to the factory where he holds a clerical position; he keeps his bouillon cup and spoon and there is plenty of boiling water accessible, so it makes a nice, nourishing drink at lunch time. —Mrs. E. B., Greensburg, Pa.

A Red Letter for Armour's Extract

We have a friend who derived more benefit (in our estimation) from Armour's Extract, than any one we have ever heard of. He is an expert machinist and is sent to all parts of the world to put up machines, such as reapers, mowers, etc. The particular trip I write of he was sent to Bulgaria, to a small village, where the accommodations were very poor. Sleep was almost out of the question and to eat the black bread, which was the principal food, was impossible. The water in all foreign countries was so bad that he always carried jars of the Extract with him. This time he not only dissolved it in hot water and drank it, but took his penknife and fed himself the extract raw. He claims it saved his life, as for four days that was all he had with him to eat or drink. He says he felt fine and did his work better than when he had been where the food was palatable and he had eaten heartily. Of course he swears by the Extract and never takes a trip now without taking a good supply with him. —Mrs. H. L., Yorktown Heights, Westchester Co., N. Y.

A New Use for Stale Bread. The Roll is Hollowed Out to Make a Serving Cup for Creamed Chicken

Don't stint the kiddies on their daily spread —give them Armour's Glendale Butterine

Making Money for the Church

"Besides selling recipes for eggless, butterless cake, we made seasoning bags to sell, for soups and such, using eight peppercorns, four cloves, six mustard seeds, one third teaspoon celery seed, four tiny sprigs each of thyme, summer savory, sweet basil, and parsley in each. This gives a blend pleasant to many tastes, and it is sufficient to flavor a soup for a large family. When the soup seems to have taken enough of the flavor the bag should be removed. To make one bag at a time would be foolish, but when enough are made to last the year out it helps out in fine shape. We also made jelly bags for sale, many ladies not having the right thickness of cloth in the house at jelly-making time."

"At Christmas time the young girls of our congregation made quite a few dollars for the church by selling boxes of preserved orange. This is their recipe: Cut six large navel oranges in slices the long way of the fruit, and boil, until tender, in three waters, pouring off the water each time. Make a syrup of five cups of sugar and one cup of water and boil the orange in this until the syrup is almost boiled away. Remove with skimmer and let stand half an hour and roll each piece in granulated sugar. The confection was packed in dainty white boxes and covered with paraffin paper. They found a very ready sale." —K. C. B.

"It has been our experience that everyday necessities in the household are better sellers than fancy nicknacks," writes a reader, "and when the social club of our church met last winter we decided to stick to them. Here are some of the things we made with the result that when we held our sale at Easter there was not one article left over and we had the sum of ninety-five dollars in the treasury."

Ice Bags

"These bags, made out of ordinary potato sacking, are for covering the cake of ice, and do much to keep down the ice bill. They are twenty-four inches long by twenty-seven inches wide and have a drawstring of common twine. They cost almost nothing and found ready sale at a quarter apiece."

Wringing Bags

"This idea we got from a trained nurse who was with us for a time, and it is a very good thing to have on hand when there is sickness. When hot cloths are to be applied it is hard to wring them out by hand as hot as the doctor would like. The bags are made of strong ticking and measure eighteen inches in width and are ten inches deep. At each end a loop the depth of the bag was stitched, through which a piece of broom handle was run when in use. To use, put the flannel into the bag, and set the bag into the pan of boiling water on the stove (first inserting the sticks). When ready, simply lift the bag and wring it by the sticks."

Carpenter's Aprons

"There has been a good deal of building done in our small town and one of our members, whose husband is a building contractor, offered to buy half a dozen carpenter's aprons if we would make them. This order has led to our making over two hundred of these aprons, as others hearing of it would want their aprons home-made rather than factory made. They are made of strong ticking, with a strap around the neck and another at the waist. In some, the straps are around the shoulders instead of the neck. Pockets are made for a rule, knife, nails, and a strap for a hammer." —Mrs. T. G. H.

Clever Fingers Made This Lounge from an Old Single Bed
ARMOUR'S SIMON PURE LEAF LARD—the best for all purposes

Where Does Your Housekeeping Money Go?

Housekeeping money to many men means the actual money required for food. Not very many husbands realize how many little expenses the housekeeping money has to take care of—little expenses that have nothing to do with food. Here are some and the Editor will be very glad if the readers will send in their own experiences in this line.

Most men smoke, and most men like to pocket a nice fresh box of matches when starting off for the day. Matches don't cost much to be sure but a fresh box each morning cuts quite a hole in the housekeeping money which is used to buy them.

Does your husband like to sit up late reading, playing chess, etc.? That sort of thing increases the light and coal bill quite a bit.

The pennies given for charity, church collections, etc., are also "extras."

Returning little courtesies—very often to "his" people—such as sending flowers, books, and occasional lunch or matinee, etc., etc., all make quite a hole in the housekeeping money.

The wear and tear of household utensils, linen, etc., means constant replenishment of one thing or another. A man may realize that his buggy or motor car has to have certain parts replaced once in a while but he is not apt to think of the pots and pans of the household side of things unless reminded.

It is a good plan to keep a few simple medicines at hand in case of sudden sickness, also a few bandages and the usual dressings required for accidents. Does your housekeeping money make provision for this?

Money for the education of the children is not generally included in the housekeeping money, but when the children get old enough to want to have their friends visit them it means little lunches, suppers, entertainments of various kinds, all of which cuts into the housekeeping money. As this is really the social side of their education it is only fair that extra provision should be made for it.

Why Eat Fruit?

It is a very good plan to find out the medicinal and curative properties of the different fruits and to make the fruit your system requires a part of your diet.

Apples, for instance, have an excellent effect on the health generally. They contain a large proportion of water and a large quantity of potash as well as of malic acid, which has valuable properties, and ether which is beneficial to the liver. Plums, too, have certain virtues and lemons are good for several forms of stomach trouble. As for grapes, they are so valuable as to form a distinctive "cure" just in themselves. They possess an enormous quantity of potash and plenty of water and they also contain sugar and salts of tartar. That all means that grapes will do much for the person who is tired and run down, whose nerves are weakened and whose organs are overworked, that they will tone and regulate the system, purify the blood and assist the different organs in performing their functions. The presence of sugar indicates that they can provide fuel for the body—the human engine—whether it be the romping child or the man whose day is filled with hard physical labor. So it follows that grapes are really a very valuable addition to our diet list.

Unfortunately, it is not always possible to have grapes on our table but wise manufacturers have found a way by which the juice of the grape may be possible at all times of the year and in every corner of the land. They have built large factories right in the very heart of the country where the best grapes grow and there the grapes are taken while the dew is still on them and their luscious fragrant deliciousness is squeezed out, poured into bottles and quickly sealed to prevent any escape of the exquisite bouquet.

Nothing is added—no water to weaken and adulterate, no sugar to sweeten, no coloring essence to deceive the eye. It is just the pure, natural juice of earth's best offering. This bottled concentration of earth's sweetness and richness with all the life and warmth of the sunshine is Armour's Grape Juice.

Jessie Tarbox Beals

Marshmallow Cake with Decoration of Marshmallows and Leaves
Cut Out of Citron Peel
Start the day right with DEVONSHIRE FARM SAUSAGE

Baked Beans—A National Dish

To many people baked beans means just one thing—baked beans, served hot or cold. To the woman, however, who is really interested in furnishing variety in diet, and this in a very economical way, baked beans offers boundless possibilities. First of all, she lays in a stock of Veribest Baked Beans—Veribest, because she knows that in this particular brand the beans are even more thoroughly cooked than she herself could do them. There are two kinds of Veribest Baked Beans, plain, and with tomato sauce, and with both the mellow richness of the bean is preserved with all its natural flavor, making it a most toothsome dish as well as nutritious and economical. Having a good stock to draw from the economical housewife proceeds to serve baked beans to her family every day for a week, varying the dish each day.

FOR MONDAY there is a New England Supper—baked beans with hot Boston brown bread. Drop the can of baked beans into hot water and boil for 20 minutes. Turn out, garnish with parsley and serve with mustard pickles.

TUESDAY, FOR LUNCH.—BEAN CROQUETTES. Drain Veribest Pork and Beans (without tomato sauce), and pass them through a colander. Measure and allow one teaspoon of dry bread crumbs to each cup of beans. Season with cayenne pepper and a little minced parsley. For a pint of the mixture, beat one egg. Save enough of the egg to dip the croquettes in, and add the remainder to the beans. Mix and form into small croquettes, or balls, then roll in fine bread crumbs. Dip them in egg and again in the crumbs, and fry in deep boiling Simon Pure Leaf Lard. Border with slices of dill pickles or sweet green peppers.

WEDNESDAY, SCHOOL LUNCHES.—BEAN SANDWICHES. Cut some thin slices from a loaf of brown bread, butter and put crisp lettuce leaves, with a teaspoon of mayonnaise, on each half of the slices, and on the others spread a layer of Armour's Veribest Pork and Beans, which have been mashed until smooth. Put the slices together and wrap each sandwich separately in paraffin paper.

THURSDAY.—BEAN CELERY SALAD. Mix one can of Veribest Pork and Beans, four tablespoons of celery cut in one eighth inch rings, two tablespoons of finely chopped onions, and one fourth cup of good boiled dressing. Marinate thoroughly, but stir slightly. Rub the salad dish with a cut clove of garlic. Arrange lettuce leaves around the salad bowl and in the center make a mound of the salad mixture, to which one fourth cup of whipped cream has been added. Garnish with stuffed olives cut in rings.

FRIDAY.—ATTRACTIVE LUNCHEON DISH. Heat one can of Veribest Pork and Beans (without tomato sauce), tossing about with fork to prevent breaking or mashing the beans. Season to taste. Serve in beet shells which have been previously prepared as follows: Wash the beets carefully, so as not to break the skins, and boil rapidly until tender. Then cover with cold water, and with the hands remove the skins. Scoop out the centers and fill the cases with the beans. Garnish with young celery leaves.

SATURDAY.—PUREE OF BEANS. To one can of Armour's Veribest Beans and Tomato Sauce add two cups of milk; boil for a few minutes and pass through a sieve. Add salt and pepper to taste, a dash of sage, dry mustard and more water if required. Strain over croutons in the tureen and sprinkle with chopped parsley.

SUNDAY NIGHT SUPPER.—BEAN LOAF. Two cups of Veribest Pork and Beans, mashed to a pulp, one fourth cup of chopped nuts, one cup of browned bread crumbs, two teaspoons of grated onion, two eggs, one half cup of cream or rich milk, one teaspoon of salt. Mix thoroughly and put into a greased bread pan. Brush with the beaten yolk of egg, milk or cream and bake one half hour. Serve with tomato sauce.

Jessie Tarbox Beals

Utilizing a Chimney Corner for a Book Case

Homely Virtues

"Scorn not the homely virtues. We are prone
To search through all the world for something new;
And yet sometimes old-fashioned things are best—
Old-fashioned work, old-fashioned rectitude,
Old-fashioned honor and old-fashioned prayer,

Old-fashioned patience that can bide its time,
Old-fashioned firesides sacred from the world,
Old-fashioned satisfaction, with enough
Old-fashioned candour and simplicity,
Old-fashioned folks that practice what they preach."

Answers to Correspondents

Please tell me the proper way to send wedding announcements. In a family where there are several young men and women do I send each a separate one?

If economy is no object send each a separate card. If you do not care to do this and they are brothers and sisters you may say "The Misses Brown" and "The Messrs. James and John Wilson."

I would like very much to be able to help other housekeepers, but I always feel that I only know the simple things of my rather humdrum life in the country.—MRS. D., OHIO.

What you know is not known to everyone, nor is what any housekeeper knows a matter of everyday use with other housekeepers. Everyone has some short cut or recipe, or personal way of doing things that would lighten the way for others. Your recommendation of butterine for instance, would carry weight with some housekeepers who had never before thought of trying it and they would be grateful always for being shown how to cut their butter bill. So with the other suggestions in your good letter from which I have taken extracts for the other pages. I want just such letters as yours. We must not forget that the younger generation of housekeepers are starting housekeeping and scanning columns like these for "the things everyone knows."

Yellow and white scheme for coming-out party.—H. M. B.

Many thanks for the nice things you say about the Cook Book. Am very glad you have enjoyed it so long. The color scheme you mention could be carried out further by wearing white dresses with yellow sashes and hair ribbons. Have yellow ices and cakes with white and yellow frosting. Egg sandwiches, potato salad garnished with hard boiled eggs halved and yellow flowers, which are quite plentiful now would all help to carry out the idea.

What is the seventh anniversary of a wedding called? and is the celebration of these anniversaries out of style? —E. G. T., BOISE CITY.

It is perfectly proper to celebrate and you can have a merry time with little expense. Have tiny woolly toy sheep for favors and serve lamb salad (made after a chicken salad recipe). Wear a woolen dress and your husband white flannels.

I belong to a little card club and have to entertain the other members one afternoon soon. Can you suggest something which is easily prepared and can be served as a lap lunch? —MRS. F. T., HUNTINGTON, W. VA.

Ham mousse in individual moulds with thin bread and butter sandwiches. Ice cream served in cantaloupe. Iced tea with a slice of lemon and Armour's Grape Juice, which needs no flavoring.

What can I put with my silverware when packing it away to keep it from tarnishing? —MRS. S.

Pack in bags of Canton flannel before putting into the drawers or boxes and place with them a few pieces of camphor gum.

Please tell me if it is proper to eat cake with the fingers or must a fork be used?

It depends on the cake. If one with a soft filling, a fork will be necessary.

Requested Recipes

FOR G. H.

Molasses Custard

Take one cup molasses (ribbon cane is the best; I have never tried corn syrup), add one half cup sugar, stir well and put on fire to boil for at least five minutes. Let cool for a short time, than add three well-beaten eggs, stirring constantly to keep the eggs from curdling. Add a tablespoonful of cornstarch. Bake in pie crust in the regular way but slowly. To keep from browning too quickly I sometimes place a tin in oven over pie.

Many thanks to Mrs. F. A. F., Jacksonville, Texas.

FOR MRS. T. H., OSWEGO, N. Y.

Boiled Bacon

Place the bacon in a saucepan with sufficient cold water to cover it. Bring the water to the simmering point and simmer gently until done (time, about half an hour for a pound for large pieces, less for smaller). Add to the water an onion with two or three cloves stuck in it, one carrot, one turnip and some sticks of celery. Skim carefully several times. When done, remove the skin and cover with browned bread crumbs.

Found Out!

When making shells for custard and lemon pies prick the crust all over with a fork before baking. Bake the shells over an inverted pie plate, then place them in pie plate as usual before filling.—Mrs. D. H., Media, Pa.

If a cake gets scorched on top when baking, grate lightly with a nutmeg grater rather than try to scrape it with a knife. You will have a better surface for frosting.—C. K., Hurley, Texas.

When your tablecloths begin to wear out make napkins out of the best parts and get a new tablecloth.

Save your old newspapers and when you sweep soak the papers in water in which a tablespoonful of ammonia has been dissolved. Squeeze out and throw the paper pulp on the floor you are about to sweep. It will keep the dust from flying and at the same time brighten the carpets.

Save all soap scraps and put them into an empty baking powder can that you have turned into a soap shaker by the help of a hammer and nail. Punch eight or ten small holes in the top and bottom, run a piece of wire from lid to bottom to hang it up by. When washing dishes shake the box in the water and you will have a nice suds.

Do not throw away the small pieces of paraffin that you take from the tops of jelly glasses. They can be melted and used again. If you do not make jelly, use them to mix with the kindling. They start a fire like coal oil. Ends of candles may be used in the same way. If the wick in the lamp is short and you are out of coal oil, fill the lamp with water. The oil will rise to the top and the wick will burn as long as there is oil to burn.

Put a tablespoonful of salt in your lamp and the blaze will be twice as bright.—C. L. E., Dayton.

A damp or slightly oily cloth is all that is necessary to polish oak furniture if it is in good condition. Marks made by wet glasses should be rubbed with a mixture of nine parts olive oil and one part paraffin.—Mrs. W., Stilesboro, Ga.

A very simple, attractive and inexpensive gift may be made by crocheting a simple edge for bath towels of the silk finished crochet cotton, and working the monogram or initial in cross stitch, using the same thread. The washrag should have a tiny edge to match.—Mrs. J. H. M., New Mexico.

My linen dress had a tear and as it was bought ready made there were no left over pieces. I drew a few threads from the under hem and darned it with these and when laundered it could scarcely be seen.—Mrs. J. E. F.

Hints for October

A Hot Drink with the School Lunch

Whether the individual drinking cup is a requirement in all public schools, or not, its use is a habit which should be encouraged. A collapsible cup takes up little room in the lunch basket. With it place one of the Armour Bouillon Cubes. At lunch time this cube dropped into a cup of hot water provides a drink of bouillon that is refreshing, stimulating and healthful.

Armour's Bouillon Cubes, chicken and beef flavor, are sold in tins of 12, 50 and 100—each cube wrapped separately in tin foil.

Fruit Out of Season

The tonic value of pure fruit juices makes them desirable all the year around, and the caloric properties of grape juice place it at the head of the list. Just now the Armour factories, in the heart of the grape-growing sections of New York and Michigan, have their presses at work extracting the pure juice from the season's luscious Concords. This juice, undiluted, unfermented and unsweetened, is immediately bottled, retaining all the delicious fragrance and flavor of the grape.

For household use there are cases of bottles in quarter-pint sizes and larger. Armour's Grape Juice is a splendid flavor for desserts and ices.

Government Inspection

Housewives realize, more than ever before, their responsibility in selecting for their families foods that are wholesome and healthful. One of the strictest Government inspections is on butterine. In using

Glendale Butterine there is a saving of fully one third over the cost of butter, and there is no question about its cleanliness, purity and wholesomeness.

Armour's Glendale Butterine is carefully wrapped and sold in paraffined cartons.

The Family Cupboard

Anyone in the family can serve on short notice a meal that is sure to please, — *if* the cupboard is well stocked from the extensive variety of Veribest Soups, Meats and Food Specialties. All are as thoroughly cooked and seasoned as in the home kitchen, and it's a simple matter to heat the contents of the cans and serve.

Best grocers in all parts of the country sell Veribest goods.

A Simple Lesson in Soup Making

The usual process of simmering meats and vegetables is so tedious and troublesome that frequently soup is omitted from the bill of fare when there is good reason for its presence. It is especially beneficial in preparing the way for the easy digestion of heavier foods. Veribest Soups are scientifically cooked and seasoned. For use, heat the soup and dilute it to the preferred consistency.

The Choice of the Many

It is the greatest satisfaction to know of one breakfast dish that is always welcomed by guests. Whether they come from North or South, they relish sweet, crisp bacon. Armour's Star Bacon is a mild sugar cure, hickory smoked, and is most delicate.

Star Bacon is sold in glass jars and paper cartons.

Keeping Household Accounts

Buying ham by the single slice is necessarily much more expensive than buying a whole ham, for there is the cost of cutting besides the waste by this method. After slices are cut from the whole ham, considerable meat will be left on the bone. These bits can be used in many ways, and the bone can be boiled with vegetables or for soup.

Armour's Star Ham is cured and smoked by special process which has given it the famous flavor.

Little But Efficient

No product is better known or more highly appreciated than the little jars of Armour's Extract of Beef. This Extract has many uses, and a little goes far in making soup stock, beef tea, flavoring the cheaper cuts of meat, gravies and vegetables.

Most druggists and grocers can supply Armour's Extract of Beef in two sizes of jars.

Women Who Succeed

To have light, flakey pastry, doughnuts that are neither heavy nor grease-soaked, and fried dishes that are just right, our successful cooks have found that the first essential is good, old-fashioned pure leaf lard, tried out in open kettles, just as our grandmothers made it. Such is Armour's Simon Pure Leaf Lard, which is sold only in pails. Best dealers can supply it.

A Luncheon Innovation

A piquant meat filling for sandwiches—one that is already prepared and requires only careful slicing—is Armour's Summer Sausage. Each of the several kinds is a careful blending of meats and seasoning. Packed in casing, they will keep indefinitely and therefore it is possible to have a supply at hand ready for any emergency.

Lightning Source UK Ltd.
Milton Keynes UK
UKHW010718120821
388748UK00001B/101

9 781006 675720